T0375536

Open When...

God's Reassurances
Through Life's
Joys and
Challenges

Noel Jansen

WESTBOW
P R E S S®
A DIVISION OF THOMAS NELSON
& ZONDERVAN

WestBow Press books may be ordered through booksellers or by contacting:

WestBow Press
A Division of Thomas Nelson & Zondervan
1663 Liberty Drive
Bloomington, IN 47403
www.westbowpress.com
844-714-3454

ISBN: 979-8-3850-1999-1 (sc)
ISBN: 979-8-3850-2000-3 (hc)
ISBN: 979-8-3850-2001-0 (e)

Library of Congress Control Number: 2024903977

Print information available on the last page.

WestBow Press rev. date: 03/20/2024

To my beautiful children. May they live fully in the assurances of God's love, protection, and provision.

Faith is the confidence that what we hope for will actually happen; it gives us assurance about things we cannot see.
—Hebrews 11:1

CONTENTS

PREFACE

The idea for this book began when, in my twenties and thirties, time was consumed with life tasks such as studies, training, moves, beginning a family, and eventually developing and growing a medical practice. During those incredibly busy years, it was difficult to find time to cultivate and nurture a strong faith. Each phase and transition brought joys, challenges, and struggles. While it would have been the perfect time to lean into my confidence in God, many times his assurances felt far off and even difficult to trust.

Looking back, I can clearly see the presence of God in times I had felt he was distant or unreachable. I am now able to appreciate how he guided me, guarded me, and walked with me through the many hills and valleys of my journey during those years and beyond. Recognizing his unfailing love and provision has grown my faith in ways I would not have fathomed years ago. It is truly a blessing to be able to trust in and rely on our faithful God.

Beginning in the early years of our marriage, my husband, Jon, and I tried to make church attendance a priority for our family. While we both felt encouraged and inspired by the messages, the busyness and demands of life seemed to sap the enthusiasm and energy from Sunday morning sermons by Monday evening. By the time midweek chaos peaked, I often couldn't fully remember the contents of the messages, let alone lean into them for reassurances and guidance.

When challenged by a certain situation, I would try to recall a message or lesson that was relevant. But with the demands on my mind and time, those efforts were often futile. Looking to the concordance, which listed words and where they could be found in the Bible, I could sometimes find scripture with the searched word or phrase in it, but there was frequently no full association to the challenge before me. I needed something that spoke more to my heart—something that would assure me of God's loving presence in my circumstances.

Joining Bible study groups to learn more about God and how to lean into trusting him was beneficial. Yet these, too, often related to only one topic at a time—and not necessarily my needs at that moment. *If only I could find a book that would address multiple topics so that I could turn to the needed encouragement at the specific time.* It was during this hectically wonderful season of life that the idea for this transcript formed.

After feeling called to write this book more than two decades ago, I had battled the enemy's tactics of self-doubt and negative self-talk for many years to be able to finally heed the divine nudges and bring the work to completion. I am eternally grateful that our heavenly Father didn't give up on me and continued to encourage me forward so that he might speak to you through these words. May all the glory, honor, and praise be to him alone.

INTRODUCTION: OPEN FIRST

Our journey through life creates a cascade of emotions. We have moments of mountaintop joys as well as deep-valley lows. We experience challenges, fears, frustrations, temptations, and an abundance of *whys* along the way. Having friends to share those times, lend a listening ear, or provide much-needed advice can bring a sense of peace and hope. Yet we don't always have a friend by our side in times of need—or we may not want to be vulnerable enough to share our current fears, thoughts, or feelings.

It's important, however, to process our emotions in a healthy way so that we don't become enslaved to them. So where else can we turn for encouragement, comfort, and peace throughout our journey? And how can we celebrate life's successes while remaining humble?

The pandemic that began in 2020 has created feelings of isolation in many of us. Whether quarantining, dodging crowds, feeling fearful while being out in public, avoiding travel, or limiting large family gatherings, a plague of separation has ensued. Snaking its way into our homes, workplaces, and communities, the weeds of isolation have begun to choke our once vibrant relationships. Many people I have spoken to describe an ongoing feeling of separation since then. As it has become more difficult to nurture relationships, there has been a global mental health crisis. At times, we may just feel so *alone*.

Yet we are never truly alone. Our Creator, God, is always there and always with us. He is a righteous God filled with truth, love, goodness, mercy, power, and generosity. As our heavenly Father, he always desires what is best for his children.

Let me pause here for a moment and acknowledge that some of you may not have had an earthly father who exemplifies these qualities, making it difficult to rely on any father anywhere. I understand that self-protective and justifiable struggle with trust. It can be an extremely difficult challenge to overcome and may create an abyss of deep pain within. But I invite you to explore a new possibility in your faith walk. Reaching a place in our hearts where we can be vulnerable with our faithful and loving God, and learning to trust him in times of need, creates an opportunity to begin healing those cavernous wounds.

Looking back on my life's journey, I realize that I have felt alone, unsure, and anxious during many challenging times. I have not seen or felt God's presence in the moment, primarily because I have been focused on pushing through and conquering life on my own. Upon deep reflection, however—sometimes years later—I have been able to see his awesome hand at work, gently guiding or carrying me through dark seasons to ultimately reach a place of hope and peace. He has repeatedly shown me that he *is* trustworthy and good and kind.

God is ready to be in a relationship with us and to love us abundantly. Unfortunately, amid the time-crunched turmoil of daily responsibilities and expectations, we often fail to look to him for guidance, peace, and hope. We miss out on the kindest and most compassionate companion we can ever have because, in the moment, we forget all about his promises. God has assured us that he is by our side in the hills, the valleys, and everywhere in between. He wants to join in celebrating our victories and crying with us in our sorrows. Intimacy with our heavenly Father materializes when we experience his faithfulness during life's challenges and joys.

Many of us turn to Google searches, books, podcasts, tutorials, or blogs to seek answers to questions we have during our ever-changing life circumstances. There are thousands of faith-based and self-help books to learn from when we have a specific challenge or want to know more about a certain topic. Yet life's commitments and chaos don't always allow us the time to read an entire book when we are seeking wisdom or advice. And finding the right podcast can take a lot of time and effort that we may not have in the moment.

To provide background, "open when" letters to friends or loved ones are written with instructions to be opened at a later time. They are a way to feel connected to that person when they cannot physically be in our presence. These personal letters deliver joy and provide encouragement. They create a connectedness between the giver and the recipient, the writer and the reader. They are a reminder that we have someone thinking about us, caring for us, and sending love through their words.

View this book as your personal set of "open when" letters. Open and read it when life circumstances align with one of the chapter titles. Turn to *Open When …* to gather brief pearls of wisdom, gain spiritual inspiration, and receive a reminder that you are not alone. Each brief chapter addresses one topic, stands alone, and can be read in less than fifteen minutes. My objective is that, when needed, the appropriate chapter will be able to speak to your heart and give you glimpses of hope and encouragement. My prayer is that, through reading the chapter and referenced scriptures, you will draw nearer to God.

As a physician, I have learned to use science to comprehend the world and people. Knowledge and wisdom lead to understanding, which is crucial as we seek opportunities for personal growth. To enhance understanding and promote reflection, there are scientific and educational components within the chapters. Through my life's journey, however, I have also learned that science cannot always explain everything we experience. Faith, too, plays a vital role in our comprehension of life circumstances, personal growth, and compassion for our world.

In my ineffective attempts to be in control and use knowledge alone to guide my life's decisions, I've found that my fallible human nature doesn't always bring the best results. When I open my heart to having faith in God and learn to trust in Jesus, however, I find freedom and beauty in a way that science cannot explain. The Word of God has provided guidance, encouragement, and hope when I most need it. The biblical references throughout the following chapters remind the reader that Jesus has encountered many of the same challenges we face today. So while I hope these pages are educational, the ultimate goals are to provide spiritual encouragement, enhance your life of faith, and bring you closer to Jesus as you walk in the assurance of God's love and grace.

At the end of each chapter are several Bible verses relating to the topic that can be read, studied, and memorized if you choose. Unless otherwise specified, they appear in the New Living Translation (NLT). They can be used as breath prayers throughout the day or put on your mirror to refer to each morning. Because the Lord speaks to many of us through music, there are also two or more contemporary Christian song titles and artists who can be impactful as you work through the specific life challenge you are facing. Listen to the songs on your way to the office, as you work around the house, or during personal reflection time. As you listen to the lyrics, pray for God to open your heart and provide wisdom and healing through the words of the chapter, the scriptures, and the music.

I have heard many people say that they don't know how to pray. Prayer is nothing more than an authentic and heartfelt conversation with God. Prayer connects us to the divine, shifts our focus to others, and allows for God's refreshing peace to permeate our parched souls. I encourage you to pray after reading each chapter, asking God to protect and guide you through the situation. If needed, each chapter concludes with a prayer to get you started. Use it to spark your personal conversation with the heavenly Father as you share your heart with him.

Open When ...: God's Reassurances through Life's Joys and Challenges is intended to be a resource in your moments or seasons of need. There are many different reasons why you may need a quick scripture reference or a voice of encouragement—times when you feel lost or alone, times when you're hurting or afraid, times when you need a spiritual pick-me-up, or times when you want to encourage someone else in need. Having walked through these situations myself does not make me an expert, but it does provide the opportunity to share my experiences and advocate for you in yours.

This book is meant to be read and absorbed one chapter at a time, in response to a specific emotion or challenge you are facing today, like a letter from a dear friend reaching out to you in your time of need. It is intended to reassure you of your faithful God's loving presence and astounding grace through every part of your journey. I encourage readers not to try to absorb more than two letters or chapters in a week to allow time for thoughtful processing and honest reflection. The goal is that each chapter will provide the beginning of inspiration, peace, and hope as you ultimately open your heart to the heavenly Father, who lovingly stands by your side, patiently waiting for his child to reach up for his hand.

My prayer is that God walks with you and speaks to you in a new way each time you reach for this book as your various life experiences require. Allow *him* to guide you to *Open When* ....

SONG FOR YOUR SOUL

- "Good Good Father" by Chris Tomlin

CHAPTER 1

When You Feel Afraid

In times of trouble, may the Lord hear your cry. May the name of the God of Jacob keep you safe from all harm.
—PSALM 20:1

L ife isn't a calm and carefree meadow through which we easily bound, stopping to watch rainbows while collecting flowers along the way. Instead, it often feels like a tortuous and rocky path of missteps and stumbles that have the potential to create pain and chaos as we try to navigate the best route forward. In fact, depending on the decisions or challenges we are facing in the moment, journeying through life can feel overwhelming and even frightening.

If you are currently being tormented by fear or in the throes of apprehension, you may be feeling numerous other emotions. Self-doubt, anger, worry, turmoil, stress, and desperation are just a few of these. As you settle in to unpack and overcome your fear, be reminded that fear is not of God. Instead, he provides loving reassurance and guidance into how we can courageously move forward in confronting our fears.

At times, fear can be protective, helping us recognize imminent danger so we may act to avoid it. Excessive fear, however, can also have many negative effects on our minds and bodies. Fear can be paralyzing. It can be counterproductive. Fear can hold us back from following our dreams and living into our divine purpose. It can cause chaos in life when all we seek is peace. Yet it is human nature to experience doubts and fears. So how can we learn to trust in God and overcome unhealthy fear when it inevitably arises?

Whatever currently causes your fear, be encouraged that you don't need to face it alone. King David in the Old Testament encountered many anxieties, fears, and uncertainties. From combatting life-threatening situations to being ridiculed to feeling insecure in his position, David always spoke openly and authentically to the heavenly Father. He felt the Lord's presence through each part of his journey. David's prayer in Psalm 20:1 might bring you strength as well: "In times of trouble, may the Lord hear your cry. May the name of the God of Jacob keep you safe from all harm." Call out to God when you feel afraid, and remember that he *is* on your side.

Former US first lady and humanitarian Eleanor Roosevelt also gave meaning and hope to the prospect of confronting our fears: "You gain strength, courage, and confidence by every experience in which you really stop to look fear in the face. You are able to say to yourself, 'I lived through this horror. I can take the next thing that comes along.' You must do the thing you think you cannot do." Self-doubt in facing challenges may create an escalation of internal turmoil and prevent us from stepping out in courage. Yet we do not need to let fear, apprehension, or anxiety control our lives.

Our fears stem from numerous sources, both internal and external. Common internal fears include the fear of failure, of rejection, of sickness, of losing a loved one, of not having enough money, or of dying. Not feeling we are on the right life path, not feeling in control, or being uncertain about the future can also create distress. We may ask ourselves, *Am I making the right job choice?* or *What if my child becomes sick?* or *Will I save enough money to retire?* While these types of questions may peak as we experience life transitions, they tend to surface repeatedly during our lives. The uncertainty can be overwhelming and provoke anxiety.

External fears relate to sources outside the body and may escalate to actual phobias. According to professionals at Northwestern University,

"Fears are common reactions to events or objects. But a fear becomes a phobia when it interferes with your ability to function and maintain a consistent quality of life."[1] Exposure to these types of triggers is uncomfortable, creates anxiety, and even causes physical changes in the body.

The body's response to fear is to become hyperalert. Heart rate and breathing accelerate. The sympathetic nervous system is activated, increasing blood flow to the muscles. The muscles tense. Glucose, which fuels movement, increases. The brain becomes less distracted and focuses on the fearful situation at hand.[2] These physiological changes prepare the body for fight or flight as methods of self-preservation.

When fear rules our thoughts, however, it can lead to ongoing anxiety. Anxiety can then consume and dominate our attention to the point of being disabling. How we perceive fear is often related to our sense of control. When we feel a situation is not under our control, it creates more anxiety than when we feel we can intentionally affect the outcome. If not in present physical danger, there are ways to calm the body, mind, and spirit in the presence of internal and external fears. Slowing our breathing, focusing on something positive, meditating, praying, and engaging in physical activity are all options to combat fear and anxiety.

Perhaps one's fear comes from a real or potential physical threat. If someone has harmed us or a loved one or if we are in a verbally or physically abusive relationship, a protective, fearful stance can occur. Friend, if you are currently sensing imminent danger, please ask for help. Don't feel that you must continue to endure this pain and suffer in silence. It takes courage to break established patterns and find the right path to the best place of safety. There are people—friends, counselors, pastors—who can help. Despite any negative self-talk, trust that you do have the bravery within you to alter your current path.

God knew that we would experience fear. In fact, I have heard that the words *do not be afraid* or *fear not* appear in the Bible 365 times! That is one passage for every day of the year. Our Creator understood that we would frequently struggle with fear and provided us numerous reassurances to combat that tendency. His promise is that when we walk faithfully with God and trust in his goodness, we do not have to be afraid. We begin by surrendering our fears to him.

Queen Esther, in the book of the Bible that bears her name, provides a biblical example for us of choosing faith over fear. As a Jew, she and all her people are to be put to death under the decree proposed by Haman, a powerful and trusted official for the king's empire. After a time of prayer and fasting, despite her insecurities and fears, Esther shows great courage in acting as a spokesperson for the Jews. She presents her perspective to the king, who grants her courageous request for mercy. In facing her fear, Esther succeeds in preserving her people and saving the Jewish nation (Esther 7:1–8:12).

You, too, can begin to face fears by trusting in God and believing he will equip you for whatever lies ahead. Moving forward despite trepidations requires faith, builds confidence, and develops character that can continue to propel you onward. It shapes who you are today and helps define who you will become tomorrow. It may necessitate a determination to ignore negative thoughts and naysayers. It sometimes requires saying yes to something you feel called to do before knowing the exact path to get there.

Jessica Honegger, author of *Imperfect Courage*, emboldens us to "go scared," knowing God will show up when we need him. If we wait until we feel confident, prepared, and unafraid, we may be waiting a very long time. When we are prayerfully confident that God has placed a passion and project on our hearts, however, success often means taking a leap of faith. Moving bravely ahead can alter the trajectory of our lives, build confidence in others who witness our courage, and change the legacy of our family.

What fear or fears are you battling right now? Naming it can be the first step to removing its power over you. Is anxiety consuming your thoughts and time or preventing you from making a difference? The enemy thrives when your fears take time and energy from leading a life of loving trust as you rest on God's assurances. It takes training, intentionality, and practice to mindfully turn away from negative thoughts and pursue God's peace.

Mindfulness—being fully conscious and focused on the present while not reacting to what is going on around us—is used as one therapy adjunct for fear and anxiety. It requires calmly and nonjudgmentally accepting one's distracting thoughts and pushing them aside to remain in the present. It allows a stillness and grounding of mind, body, and spirit. Once in a mindful state, we can prayerfully relinquish our anxieties and fears to God. (More details on practicing mindfulness can be found in the appendix.)

Take a moment to visualize a mother hen protecting her chicks from danger. Sensing a threat, she calls to them, spreading her wings so they may find safe shelter from peril when they come close to her. She selflessly sacrifices her own body as protection if necessary. Being in the presence of their mother hen brings the chicks feelings of safety and security. They know she values them above all else and will never abandon them.

Friend, know that God loves *you* and offers protection for *you* in that same way. Remember that our Father in heaven values you above all else and has selflessly sacrificed his Son for your protection. He will never abandon you. However, your role in this protective relationship is crucial. Just as the chicks must obey their mother hen's call to them so she can provide safe refuge, so must we obey our Father's call to come to him in times of fear. Being close to him provides protection from the storms of life and can bolster courage so we can learn to dance in the rain.

Allow God to bring strength and courage in the face of life's many hazards and amid your greatest fears. Begin to envision his protective wings covering you right now. Name your biggest fear, anxiety, or uncertainty and tuck it high up under one of those enormously safe and compassionate wings. Then release that fear and fully surrender it to your kind, loving, and gracious Father, knowing he will guard you and care for you through this struggle or as you courageously step out in an uncertain direction.

Slowly breathe in his Spirit, allowing the truth of his love and protection to meet you exactly where you are. Now breathe out any anxious thoughts that keep you from God. Calmly refuse to take that fear back from under his wing and let the Lord's reassuring presence wash over you. Any time you feel the fear or anxiety start to meander back into your thoughts, return to him and his wings. Mindfully allow God's voice to quiet your spirit and soothe your soul. Live courageously into all you are created to be. Choose peace over panic. Choose faith over fear.

VERSES TO ENCOURAGE YOU

He will cover you with his feathers, and under his wings you will find refuge.

—Psalm 91:4

Peace I leave with you; my peace I give you … Do not be troubled and do not be afraid.

—John 14:27 (New International Version, or NIV)

For I hold you by your right hand—I, the Lord your God. And I say to you, "Don't be afraid. I am here to help you."

—Isaiah 41:13

For the Lord your God is living among you. He is a mighty savior. He will take delight in you with gladness. With His love, He will calm all your fears.

—Zephaniah 3:17

SONGS FOR YOUR SOUL

- "Peace Be Still" by Hope Darst
- "I Will Fear No More" by the Afters
- "No Fear" by Kari Jobe
- "Stand in Your Love" by Josh Baldwin

6

A CONVERSATION WITH GOD

Dear God,

I feel uncertain and alone. You say, "Do not be afraid," but I feel it's beyond my control. I don't understand why I am in this position, God, yet I know you are my refuge and my protector. I need to feel your strength and shield, Father. Please help me be open to your love and comfort that reminds me I am never truly alone. As you are calling me to move forward in courage, allow me to feel your calming presence and to rest in the shelter of your loving wings. Amen.

NOTES

CHAPTER 2

When You Feel like Complaining

Why am I discouraged? Why is my heart so sad? I will put my hope in God! I will praise him again—my Savior and my God!

—PSALM 42:5

How often does it feel as if life isn't going your way? No matter what you do, no matter how hard you try, failure seems to prevail. Maybe it is a poor work review, the kids not picking up after themselves, not having enough time to prepare for an important meeting, having a partner who isn't hearing you, or even just a bad hair day. While the natural tendency may be to complain, it's rarely a beneficial option. Isaiah Hankel, author of *The Science of Intelligent Achievement*, states, "Never waste a second of your life complaining. Complaining doesn't solve problems, it attracts them. The more you complain, the more problems you'll have."

None of us want more problems, right? Life seems to provide plenty of challenges, and it never seems that *everything* is going right at the same time. And the periods when nothing seems to go right? Well, those are downright exhausting. Trudging through the muck and mire, we may then be tempted to have a pity party for ourselves, thinking, *Why me? Why do these troubles always happen to me? Why do other people seem to sail easily through life and I only have a stream of difficulties? Why, God? Why?*

Know that it is OK to ask God those questions. He wants to hear about not only your love and awe for him but also your deepest troubles. In the Old Testament, David had an intimate relationship with the Lord, bringing him both praises and concerns. God did not love or care for David any less when he expressed his woes: "Why am I discouraged? Why is my heart so sad? I will put my hope in God! I will praise him again—my Savior and my God!" (Ps. 42:5). You, too, can deepen your relationship with God by bringing him your toughest and most heartfelt concerns through prayer.

It's easy to fall into the trap of feeling sorry for ourselves when we think about all the difficulties and obstacles against us. And unfortunately, we tend to ruminate on just those problems, losing sight of anything encouraging in our lives. This negative focus may lead to a downward spiral of our mood, outlook, productivity, and relationships. As we complain to our spouse, best friend, sibling, or someone else, we give voice to the negativity, providing the opportunity for it to escalate.

Life, however, is a matter of perspective. Do we see the glass as half empty or half full? Shawn Achor, an American happiness researcher and founder of the consulting and training business GoodThink, writes, "I would suggest a different way of looking at the metaphorical glass. We get so focused on ourselves and what's inside the glass—our physical possessions, daily moods, failures, and triumphs—and we can argue forever about the merits of being an optimist or a pessimist. Ultimately, however, the contents of the glass don't matter; what's more important is to realize there's a pitcher of water nearby. In other words, we have the capacity to refill the glass, or to change our outlook."[1]

Not only do we have the capacity to refill the glass but we also have an advocate to help us do just that. In the New Testament book of John, Jesus shouted to the nearby crowds, "Whoever believes in me, as Scripture has said, rivers of living water will flow from within them" (John 7:38, NIV). You see, God provides a limitless abundance of healing water in that pitcher, friend—water to revive, refresh, and nourish our souls during the most difficult times. We simply must remember that the pitcher is within our grasp.

The unfortunate part about troubled times is that we often forget the many great favors that God has done for us in the past and even our current blessings. How often has God provided exactly what we need at precisely the right time? How many wonderful small gifts do we take for granted each day? If we force ourselves to think back to a time when life has been less disappointing, can we recall some positives?

Maybe it's having a sturdy roof over our heads, a loving family, a trusted friend who accepts us for who we are, sufficient food on the table, good health, the ability to learn and better ourselves, the joy of a special hobby, a devoted pet, or the beauty of the world around us. Why, when we feel like complaining, do we forget all those things and more? Why do we forget to reach out for that pitcher of God's healing water to fill our glass?

It's a natural tendency to feel caught up in the moment and to risk being swept up in a tumultuous sea of negativity. To counteract those thoughts, one of the best exercises is to list three to five things for which we are grateful. Complaining and gratitude cannot exist in the same space. If you are feeling this type of frustration or are in a downward slump right now, please stop reading and take a few minutes to begin your gratitude list. When a negative thought enters your mind, shift the focus to a current or recent blessing. Write those blessings on paper and engrave them in your heart. Seriously, pick up a pen and begin right now. Let the positives take hold of your attention throughout the exercise.

Now continue to journal a thank-you to God each day, even on those that seem awful. It is amazing how living life with an attitude of gratitude can help pull us out of a funk. By appreciating some of life's little things, we realize that, even though not everything is just right, many parts of our life may be very right. Remember: even during the midst of life's most violent storms, there are flashes of light providing glimmers of hope.

Daily we have a choice about what type of attitude we will have for that day. We can opt to focus on the negative, or we can decide to be grateful. As author Barbara Johnson has written, "We can choose to gather to our hearts the thorns of disappointment, failure, loneliness, and dismay due to our present situation, or we can gather the flowers of God's grace, unbounding love, abiding presence, and unmatched joy."[2] I love the visual of a beautiful bouquet filled with God's gifts to us, don't you?

Look back at the list you have just created. As you recognize some positives in life right now, begin to gather those joys for your bouquet. It is impossible to be thankful and complain at the same time, right? So focusing on and appreciating something positive, whether big or small, is a first step that can begin a colossal turnaround in perspective. Build the bouquet. Reach for that pitcher of life-sustaining water that God abundantly provides. Choose gratitude.

VERSES TO ENCOURAGE YOU

Oh, how sweet the light of day, and how wonderful to live in the sunshine! Even if you live a long time, don't take a single day for granted. Take delight in each light-filled hour.
—Ecclesiastes 11:7–8 (The Message: The Bible in Contemporary Language, or MSG)

Thank God for this gift too wonderful for words!
—2 Corinthians 9:15

Friends, don't complain about each other. A far greater complaint could be lodged against you, you know. The judge is standing just around the corner.
—James 5:9 (MSG)

This is the day the Lord has made. We will rejoice and be glad in it.

—Psalm 118:24

SONGS FOR YOUR SOUL

- "Grateful" by Elevation Worship
- "Bring the Rain" by MercyMe
- "Great Is Thy Faithfulness" by Jordan Smith

A CONVERSATION WITH GOD

Dear God,

I am stuck in this place of frustration and feel trapped in a pattern of complaining. May the Holy Spirit shift my focus, God. Give me the ability to get past my current annoyances and see the bigger picture, Father. I am thankful today for _____. As I focus on this positive, remove from me the inclination to complain. Help me see the silver lining in this situation, in this day, and in my life. Give me the perspective to see your light illuminating my blessings so that I may live with an attitude of gratitude. Amen.

NOTES

CHAPTER 3

When You Need to Forgive Someone

But love your enemies, do good to them, and lend to them
without expecting to get anything back. Then your reward
will be great. Be merciful, just as your Father is merciful.
—LUKE 6:35-36

As broken humans, people can be very hurtful. At times, they make comments or take vicious actions with the intent to harm. Other times, we feel wounded when someone says or does something without even realizing the impact it will have. It may be treating us unfairly, gossiping about us, criticizing our work, being left out of a special event, saying harsh words, judging us by how we look or dress, or even ridiculing us because of our faith. Are you experiencing this type of wound right now? Are you wrestling with the choice to fester or forgive?

Whatever the form of attack, these abuses are emotionally, and at times may be physically, painful. Author Sue Monk Kidd speaks to the challenge of moving past the pain and growing in forgiveness. "I learned a long time ago that some people would rather die than forgive. It's a strange truth, but forgiveness is a painful and difficult process. It's not something that happens overnight. It's an evolution of the heart." The hardening of the heart begins when we, as sensitive human beings, are wounded in childhood, and it progresses through a lifetime of offenses.

While hurt feelings often rule the teenage years, especially when social media seems to provide an invitation to criticize, the pain can linger far into adulthood. Whoever coined the saying "Forgive and forget" must not have had a very long memory. It feels almost impossible to forget a perceived wrong quickly, and the resulting pain can gnaw at us, creating a gaping wound of both physical and psychological damage. Remembering the event can provide an opportunity to learn from the situation and do our best to prevent it again in the future. Dwelling on the offense, however, causes an internal festering that has the potential to damage our very soul.

God doesn't tell us that we must forget when we have been offended, but he does teach us how to forgive. He knows our woundedness can create a difficult road to ongoing problems and heartache. He doesn't want that for us. As tempting as it may be, revenge is never a good option. We need to trust, instead, that the Lord is our avenger and will ultimately right any wrongs we have experienced.

Jesus tasks us with an even greater challenge in Luke 6:35–36 (NIV): "But love your enemies, do good to them, and lend to them without expecting to get anything back. Then your reward will be great. Be merciful, just as your Father is merciful."

Wow! You may not feel like doing any of those things right now. Whoever has wounded you certainly doesn't deserve your mercy and forgiveness. Or do they? Jesus promises that in showing kindness and love to those who have harmed us, we will reap a godly gift. So how is it possible to move beyond the pain you're feeling in this moment to reach a heart of forgiveness?

The closer a person is to us, the more deeply their criticisms can wound. Holding on to the grudge, however, is like a leaky faucet that erodes our relationship drop by drop until one of two things happens. If the leak breaks loose or if the woundedness comes to a head, an outburst can result, with an avalanche of explosive anger adding long-term damage to an already difficult situation.

On the other hand, if a slow leak persists, it can result in mold and rotting, or bitterness, in the relationship and in our heart. A hardened spirit can lead to building emotional brick walls that distance us not only from the one who has hurt us but from other people as well. It works against the needed heart transformation Kidd describes. Remaining angry and bitter can potentially have a negative effect on many, or even all, of our personal relationships. That's when we need to ask ourselves, *Is it really worth it?*

Can you feel the effects of resentment in your heart, mind, body, and spirit? Holding on to bitterness from a past hurt is like allowing a toxin to poison your very being. Research studies have confirmed that there are detrimental effects on our bodies when we harbor anger and bitterness. From headaches to abdominal issues to skin disorders to high blood pressure, depression, anger, and resentment—these take a huge toll on our health. On the other hand, learning to forgive has been scientifically shown to be beneficial.

Fred Luskin, PhD, director of the Stanford University Forgiveness Projects and author of *Forgive for Good*, describes the many beneficial physical effects of forgiveness. Forgiving other people boosts the immune system, reduces depression and anxiety, lowers blood pressure, and improves sleep patterns. It is a practice that can be learned, and it is a powerful path to spiritual and physical healing. In the process of forgiving someone, we begin to feel less stress and experience an inner calm that can never occur with the persistent poison of resentment.

In the book *Forgive and Forget: Healing the Hurts We Don't Deserve*, Lewis Smedes teaches four steps to the process of forgiveness. By working through hurt and hate, healing, and coming together, we are able to journey to a place of peace.[1] As we reach that point of acceptance, we learn that forgiveness is not a gift to our offender. After all, they may not even realize the impact their words or actions have had on us, or they may not care. Forgiving others frees *us*, you and me, from the bondages of hate, resentment, and emotional pain. It provides physical and emotional healing, allowing a sense of freedom in the mind. Forgiveness lets the needed transformation of our hearts begin. Reaching a point of being able to forgive, however, can require a long and tortuous journey.

Picture Jesus as he modeled unfathomable forgiveness, praying for those who severely beat him and nailed him to the cross. God avenged and overcame that painful death when Jesus walked out of the grave.

Although your pain may not be physical, the wounds you feel have the potential to slowly kill your spirit. It will take strength and intentionality to move beyond the pain and begin to forgive. When we forgive, the Holy Spirit moves through the depths of our being, making our hearts feel lighter. When we permit his light to shine in us, God's permeating presence of peace begins to settle our souls.

Friend, know that you are not alone in your pain and woundedness. There is no shame in being the target of another's attack or in having hurt feelings. It's important to fully process the incident to objectively gain understanding. Don't force yourself to try to forget the event, knowing this may never be possible. Rather than allowing it to fester in your heart, however, tuck it away as a learning experience. Know that forgiveness doesn't happen overnight and allow yourself grace through the process. It may take days, months, or even years to reach a point of being ready to relinquish the existing pain and fully forgive.

This journey won't likely be an easy one, friend. You may be hurting enough now that you can take only the first step, but at least that is progress in the right direction. Pray for God to give you the wisdom, strength, and fortitude to continue the process. Allow him to help repair the leaky faucet of anger, pain, and shame so that restoration in your relationship can begin. In allowing your heart to be softened, you may eventually find that following Jesus's instructions to pray for and do good to your perpetrator brings an unfathomable sense of peace. Knowing that healing and an evolution of your heart are on the horizon makes the current effort worth persisting to compassionately offer grace and mercy. Your transformed heart is just the beginning of your heavenly reward.

VERSES TO ENCOURAGE YOU

Be kind and compassionate to one another, forgiving each other, just as Christ God forgave you.
—Ephesians 4:32

Love ... is not easily angered, it keeps no record of wrongs.

—1 Corinthians 13:5

For if you forgive men when they sin against you, your heavenly Father will also forgive you.

—Matthew 6:14

Make allowances for each other's faults, and forgive anyone who offends you. Remember the Lord forgave you, so must forgive others.

—Colossians 3:13

SONGS FOR YOUR SOUL

- "Forgiveness" by Matthew West
- "Losing" by Tenth Avenue North
- "Forgiveness" by TobyMac featuring Lecrae

A CONVERSATION WITH GOD

Dear God,

I am feeling hurt and confused. How can someone upset me like this and not seem to know or care? I realize this anger and resentment I'm feeling will only lead to more pain. Yet here I am, replaying the hurt in my mind and feeling more and more offended and irritated. You call us to love and forgive one another. Give me the strength and courage to open my heart to the possibility of forgiving. Help me let go of the painful memory, move on, and choose peace. Grant me a pure heart, oh Lord, so that I may honor you. Amen.

19

 NOTES

CHAPTER 4

When You Feel Angry

Don't be quick to fly off the handle. Anger boomerangs.
You can spot a fool by the lumps on his head.
—ECCLESIASTES 7:9 (MSG)

What makes you angry? When are you most likely to fly off the handle? And how do you react when these situations arise? Do you yell, stew inside, plan revenge? Do you get over it and move on, or do you hold a grudge? People have many ways of dealing with anger, but some are more destructive than others. For instance, unkind words spoken in anger can never be taken back. But they can be a poison that destroys our friendships and relationships.

Chicago therapist Susan L. Adler warns, "If you spend your time hoping someone will suffer the consequences for what they did to your heart, then you're allowing them to hurt you a second time in your mind." Devoting time to the negativity that surrounds anger, whether justified or not, takes away from energy that can be spent on improving oneself, building relationships, and seeking joy. Rather than lashing out, we must instead work to protect our mind, value our time, and learn to cope with anger in constructive ways.

In the Old Testament, King Solomon shares wise counsel about the risks of unfiltered, angry encounters: "Don't be quick to fly off the handle. Anger boomerangs. You can spot a fool by the lumps on his head" (Eccles. 7:9, MSG). You may not feel ready or able to have a calm conversation in moments of anger, but take heart that it is a response that can be learned. As with exercising any muscle, the choice to defuse an angry encounter takes practice.

What happens physiologically when we become angry? The amygdala is the emotion center of the brain, controlling the fight-or-flight response to perceived threats or attacks, gauging them in a fraction of a second. This innate pathway allows us to react quickly, without thinking, for self-preservation. The frontal lobe is the reasoning center of the brain, which processes perceived threats and develops logical responses. But this pathway takes a few seconds to navigate. When we lash out quickly in anger, we are allowing our emotion center (amygdala) rather than our reasoning center (frontal lobe) to rule our actions. For this reason, counting to ten before responding creates the opportunity to de-escalate emotions. Then our brain can fully process an event and determine the best response.

God has given us all our emotions, even anger. There is no sin in feeling angry. As a matter of fact, righteous anger, which may occur when we witness an injustice, can be an igniting spark for change. The way we deal with anger, however, is our own choosing. Losing our temper will seldom solve any problem and can lead to aberrant behavior, which is much more likely to make matters worse. Stewing about it will only lead to more anger and frustration. The best way to handle most of these situations is to peacefully talk through them. It may mean exercising the count-to-ten rule. It may mean waiting several minutes (or hours or days) to cool down to the point that we can think and speak calmly.

The American Psychological Association recommends several strategies to remain calm in the face of anger.[1] First, check yourself. You need to become in tune with your physical and emotional responses as your anger escalates. Try to identify the warning signs that you're becoming frustrated and then step away from the situation.

Second, don't dwell on the incident, but learn to let go of the past. Try to focus on something you appreciate about the person who has made you angry to defuse and redirect the negative energy. Focusing on a positive direction gives us time to shift focus and blow off some steam.

The third strategy is to change our thought patterns through a technique known as cognitive restructuring: replacing negative, anger-filled thoughts with more positive ones. Perhaps instead of saying, "He has ruined everything!" think, *Well, that is cold and rude, but it isn't the end of the world.* It also helps to avoid all-or-nothing words, such as *always* and *never.* Thoughts such as *She always does this to me!* only escalate emotions. Instead, we can use reasoning to prevent anger from becoming irrational.

The fourth strategy is to relax. Slow breathing, positive imagery, meditation, prayer, and focused muscle relaxation are all ways to encourage our bodies and minds to soften. Using these methods regularly creates muscle memory, a pattern that our body can then settle into more easily when emotions begin to flare. As with everything in life, it becomes easier with practice.

Numbers 14:18 reminds us, "The Lord is slow to anger and filled with unfailing love, forgiving every kind of sin and rebellion." As we work toward sanctification and becoming more like Jesus, we, too, need to strive to be slow to anger and readily forgive those who have offended or wounded us. This can be a slow and sometimes painful process, but we are not on this journey alone.

We are called to emulate the compassion that God displays for us in our dealings with others (Luke 6:36). Jesus modeled this compassion in his response to those who beat and murdered him: "Father, forgive them, for they don't know what they are doing" (Luke 23:34). Imagine the immense strength, self-control, and intentional quieting of the mind Jesus needed to respond in such a noble way. Releasing anger and moving toward forgiveness requires a similar calming of the mind and spirit. You may not feel that you can do it, but *all* things are possible with Christ.

What activities help calm you? Maybe take a walk, go for a run, meditate, practice yoga, listen to some favorite music, read, or play with a loving pet. Whatever your proven method is, do it! Then calmly approach the person and situation without flying off the handle.

Don't put off the opportunity to reconcile when anger is affecting a relationship. Once you have control of your emotions, do it quickly and directly.

God desires for us to exercise self-control, and this requires practice. Make today the day that you work to strengthen that muscle. Try to emulate Jesus's response of thoughtful and calm words as people tried to antagonize him and then battered his body. Your response to the rage you're currently feeling is a great opportunity to live out the final fruit of the Holy Spirit, self-control (Gal. 5:22–23). Use the techniques above or whatever works for you and then pray for a calm response in this emotionally charged situation. Envision being in your happy place and allow God's peace and calm to blanket you in these moments of frustration, bringing tranquility in the face of anger. He alone, in his mighty power and quiet wisdom, will give you the necessary strength when you relinquish control of your emotions and trust in him.

VERSES TO ENCOURAGE YOU

But the Holy Spirit produces this kind of fruit in our lives: love, joy, peace, patience, kindness, goodness, faithfulness, gentleness, and self-control.
—Galatians 5:22–23

Love ... is not easily angered, it keeps no record of wrongs.
—1 Corinthians 13:5

A fool gives vent to his anger, but a wise man keeps himself under control.
—Proverbs 29:11

A gentle answer turns away wrath, but a harsh word stirs up anger.
—Proverbs 15:1

Everyone should be quick to listen, slow to speak, and slow to become angry, for man's anger does not bring about the righteous life that God desires.

—James 1:19–20

SONGS FOR YOUR SOUL

- "No Matter What" by Kerrie Roberts
- "Anchor" by Skillet

A CONVERSATION WITH GOD

Dear God,

I am frustrated and upset. My initial thought is to lash out or get even. I know these are not godly responses, and I will regret those words and actions later. Fill me with your peace that surpasses understanding and help me calm myself now and in future situations, Father. Please give me the fruit of self-control in my anger. Rather than lashing out, help me weigh my words carefully before I speak. Lord, mercifully allow me to be a vessel of peace and not of pain. In Jesus's name, I pray. Amen.

NOTES

CHAPTER 5

When You Feel Alone

Come close to God, and he will come close to you.
—JAMES 4:8

P oet and novelist Sylvia Plath articulately describes *aloneness* as a perspective of self-consciousness that is appalling and overpowering. *Loneliness* has been defined as sadness because one has no friends or company. In reality, however, loneliness is more a state of mind that can occur even when surrounded by other people. Moving to a new town, starting a new job, taking a stand that is opposite of what those near to you believe, going through a divorce, or experiencing the death of someone close to you can all lead to feeling alone.

My heart aches for you as you navigate this pain. Whatever the cause of your isolation, it can be overcome. So many things in life try to pull the focus away from the truth of God's unconditional love for you. But your story doesn't end with this current situation. Jesus has gone to the cross and died for you so that you may have a close and loving relationship with God, the heavenly Father. That, my friend, is truth.

In this age of social media, it is ironic that the more social we become on these platforms, the more time we are actually isolated from other humans in our lives. In fact, we are said to be in a "loneliness epidemic," which many feel is fueled by the overuse of gadgets and social media.

While positive experiences on social media may create a momentary feeling of elation, negative experiences tend to have longer-lasting effects. Studies conducted by Brian Primack of the American Society for Clinical Investigation and others conclude that negative experiences on social media are linked to both depression and greater social isolation.[1]

In addition to depression, loneliness is linked to health issues, such as increased stress, cardiovascular disease, poor decision-making, decreased memory, less sleep, premature aging, and substance abuse.[2] Quarantines and isolation during the coronavirus pandemic of 2020 have led to epidemic proportions of loneliness and depression. With so many detrimental effects, it becomes increasingly important to recognize loneliness in ourselves to take countermeasures. So how can we combat these feelings when they occur?

One option when feeling alone is to take yourself into a social environment, such as a coffeehouse or a shopping mall. Even brief interactions with the employees, combined with being around other people, can begin to lift your spirits. Contact a close friend to arrange a meeting. It isn't necessary to have an abundance of friends; quality interactions are the goal. Volunteer with a community service organization that is meaningful to you. This not only promotes a feeling of self-worth but also provides an opportunity to connect with other like-minded people. And last but certainly not least, open your Bible.

Jesus's brother James has penned a New Testament book filled with practical tips for following a life of faith. James says that God is always present and ready to draw near to us when we seek him. It requires intentional action on our part to feel his presence and comprehend that we are not alone.

God knows there will be many times in life we will feel abandoned, isolated, and uncertain of his presence. We are reminded throughout the Bible, however, that we are never truly alone, and he is aware of all our sorrows (Ps. 56:8). God is with us in our joy and in our suffering. He promises to meet us, guide us, and carry us through trials and the pain of feeling alone. Our heavenly Father assures he will strengthen and help us (Isa. 41:10). Do we believe it?

Have you ever given God the chance to fill your heart when you're feeling alone? While you may know that is a possible starting place, it may not be the first, second, or even third place to naturally turn. Perhaps this is the time for you to give God a chance by letting go of the aloneness and trusting him. Can I encourage you right now to sit palms up with an open heart and ask God to make himself known to you in a meaningful way? Rest in this posture of openness for several minutes, sharing with God the pain and reality of your current situation. Allow the truths of his unconditional love and merciful grace to fill you in this moment and to bring you hope.

It hurts my heart to know that you are in pain and feeling alone. As I send a virtual hug your way, I am also praying that God will make his presence known and felt by all who read this chapter. His favor and kindness are available for everyone who seeks him, and that includes you. Continue to pray for God to give you the courage to lay down your loneliness, look past your current reality, and open your heart to him. He desires to be your Comforter. He longs to bring you hope. Tuck yourself deep within the shelter of his loving arms and allow his warmth and unbounding love to permeate your soul. Scripture assures that he is with you and will carry you through. Trust God to keep his word; he always does.

VERSES TO ENCOURAGE YOU

I will never fail you. I will never abandon you.
—Hebrews 13:5

Remain in me, and I will remain in you. For a branch cannot produce fruit if it is severed from the vine, and you cannot be fruitful unless you remain in me.
—John 15:4

And be sure of this: I am with you always, even to the end of the age.
—Matthew 28:20

Do not be afraid or discouraged. For the Lord your God is with you wherever you go.

—Joshua 1:9

SONGS FOR YOUR SOUL

- "I Am Not Alone" by Kari Jobe
- "Never Walk Alone" by Hillsong Worship
- "Thank God I Do" by Lauren Daigle

A CONVERSATION WITH GOD

Dear God,

I know that you have promised to never abandon me, but I feel completely alone. As I sink further into this abyss of loneliness, it seems impossible to find a way out. I want to find a way out! Breathe your Spirit into me now, God, so I can feel the truth of your presence. Give me a sense of belonging. Help me see the next steps I need to take to feel less isolated. And give me the courage to follow through as I trust in you. Amen.

NOTES

CHAPTER 6

When You Are Tempted to Be Untruthful

May integrity and honesty protect me, for I put my hope in you.

—PSALM 25:21

Lies. Deceit. Perfidy. Dishonesty. We have all been victims of untruths spoken to us or about us. When lied to, we may feel insulted, angry, or betrayed. Some people view lying as a way to avoid confrontations, but it creates a stain on our reputation that is difficult to remove. Deceit paves the way for broken relationships in both our personal and professional lives. Unfortunately, lying or stretching the truth is an all-too-common temptation.

If we tell the boss that we have completed the required task, even if we haven't, at least we won't have to deal with the consequences right then. If we tell a friend that we are staying home when we are really planning to go out with another friend, at least it won't hurt their feelings. If we fib to our partner about our shopping spree, maybe we can recoup the money before they notice. If we lie about who we are and what we believe, maybe that new neighbor will like the artificial us. If we stretch the truth to a friend or tell a little white lie, maybe they will think better of us than if they know the real story. Do any of these situations resonate?

It is hard to be real, isn't it? It's hard to put ourselves in a vulnerable place, not knowing what the response may be. Psalm 25 reminds us, though, that truthfulness and reliability can provide protection, God's protection: "May integrity and honesty protect me, for I put my hope in you" (Ps. 25:21). We are encouraged to live a righteous life, including telling the truth, even when that truth is difficult to share.

Rationalizing deception may make it seem OK because the situation will be better in the short term. But the short term comes to an end quickly, and then we are left dealing with the consequences. When the truth comes out, the situation typically is far worse than if we had been honest in the first place. To delay facing the truth doesn't change the truth, and at some point, we must own up to it. Then we also must deal with the fact that we initially lied and the consequences that it brings. In reality, when an untruth is revealed, the end result is typically far more damaging.

When we lie to someone, they lose their faith and trust in us. They are less likely to believe us the next time. At work, they may not trust us for the next project or believe we are worthy of the promotion. When friends feel betrayed, they may be less likely to want to spend time with us. Once lost, we must work to earn back that trust, which can be extremely difficult to do. Sometimes relationships are permanently damaged.

Think about the guilt we feel after telling a partial truth or a fib. Guilt can lead to physical symptoms and anxiety. The horrible feelings we get in the pit of our stomachs are a sign that the Holy Spirit is trying to lead us to a better decision. We have the choice in that moment whether to proceed with the deception.

In *Psychology Today*, author Suzanne Degges-White discusses the thirteen essential traits of good friends.[1] Trustworthiness and honesty top the list. Being honest shows respect for yourself and others. It displays maturity and authenticity, which are important qualities in all relationships. It develops a sense of trust among family, friends, and colleagues. When we show integrity and are truthful, others are encouraged to be honest as well. As a result, we develop a genuine, caring, and trustworthy network of people in our lives.

The Bible is very clear, all the way back to the Ten Commandments, that lying is wrong in God's eyes. For some of us with rebellious spirits, being told not to do something leads to the question "Why?" and can seemingly push us more in the direction of undesirable behavior. While stretching the truth and telling little white lies may seem harmless, these choices are turning us away from others and God. Because he understands how devastating the consequences can be, God wants us to make a better choice. He hungers for us to be honest with him, with ourselves, and with others. Our loving Father knows this will provide the best path to healthy and fruitful relationships.

To overcome this temptation takes intentionality. We must ask ourselves why we lie and to whom. We should reflect on the driving force. Are we trying to impress others? Afraid of being caught? Trying to make excuses for a pattern of behavior? We must accept that we are all flawed humans incapable of perfection. And we don't need to pretend otherwise. Each of us has unique gifts, so it isn't helpful to compare ourselves with others. Yes, let's try to be the best versions of ourselves and then let others see the unveiled truth of who we are.

Being straightforward in communication provides a healthy foundation in relationships, both personally and professionally. Trying to build on false pretenses or exaggerations of our talents leads to unrealistic and unattainable expectations. It is a recipe for ultimate failure and potential disaster. Honesty allows us to create realistic goals within our abilities and provides a good example to follow.

As difficult as it is at times, tactful and gentle honesty is always best. Overcoming the temptation of deception and having the courage to speak honestly bolsters self-confidence. It also makes it easier to be truthful in the future. Own up to mistakes and poor judgment. There may be consequences for actions if we have done something wrong, but our integrity remains intact. People will probably recognize that we could have lied or shifted blame but didn't. They may not agree with what we have done, but chances are that they will get past it more quickly. And they will respect us for our honesty.

Can I encourage you to pray before you communicate again with someone to whom you may be tempted to be dishonest or stretch the truth? Ask for courage and integrity as you are vulnerable in revealing the true situation and the true you. Pray for God to give you peace in being warmly authentic and having integrity. Allow the Holy Spirit to blanket you with the determination to be noble, right, and pure in all your exchanges.

God will ultimately honor you as you honor him with truthful words. It is in that honoring communion that we draw closer to our heavenly Father and thereby build deep relationships with others based on heartfelt authenticity. Living an unpretentious life will benefit you and others, my friend. Valuable, genuine, and supportive friendships await on the other side of your honesty. Keep it real.

VERSES TO ENCOURAGE YOU

I know, my God, that you test the heart and are pleased with integrity.

—1 Chronicles 29:17

Don't lie to each other, for you have stripped off your old sinful nature and all its wicked deeds.

—Colossians 3:9

The tongue that brings healing is a tree of life, but a deceitful tongue crushes the spirit.

—Proverbs 15:4

Teach me your way, O Lord, and I will walk in your truth; give me an undivided heart.

—Psalm 86:11

SONGS FOR YOUR SOUL

- "If We're Honest" by Francesca Battistelli
- "We Won't Be Shaken" by Building 429

A CONVERSATION WITH GOD

Dear God,

I want to be honest with people, but I am sometimes tempted to stretch the truth or even tell a lie. Give me the courage to be authentic and vulnerable. I know that honesty is the best policy, but in the moment, I don't always make that best decision. Lord, I want to be trustworthy. I want to show integrity to those around me. Help me see and speak the truth. When I am tempted otherwise, please send the Holy Spirit to persuade me to make a better choice. In Jesus's name, I pray. Amen.

NOTES

CHAPTER 7

When You Are Tempted to Be Unkind

Kind words are like honey—sweet to the soul and healthy for the body.

—PROVERBS 16:24

W hy are we sometimes cruel to other people? What prompts us to criticize, call someone a name, talk behind their back, or look down on them? While this type of behavior is unfortunately typical in teenagers, many adults feel the same temptations to be unkind. Our desire to feel worthy, accepted, or part of a group can lead to us ridiculing others. While we may feel better in the moment, unkind words often have a way of backfiring.

Kindness and compassion, on the other hand, are attributes that are difficult to fault. Relationship consultant and inspirational speaker Barbara De Angelis says, "Love and kindness are never wasted. They always make a difference. They bless the one who receives them, and they bless you, the giver." Yet in day-to-day life, we sometimes fall into the trap of joining the group gossip or not treating people the way we want to be treated. What leads to this behavior?

The social comparison theory states that we determine our own social and personal worth based on how we compare with others.[1] To feel better about ourselves, we tend to make downward comparisons.

These are judgments in which we look down on someone else to make ourselves feel better. We begin to believe that we will feel better about ourselves if we make others feel less important, less beautiful, or less cool than we are. Our own insecurities, therefore, fuel the temptation to be unkind.

And when we see others being cruel, it's all too easy to join in. To be accepted or to feel part of the group, we go along with it. We participate in it. We promote the problem. This innate desire to fit in can lead to unhealthy, unfounded, and unconscious biases, such as racism, sexism, ageism, and heterosexism. Self-doubt consequently drives much of the cruelty in our world today. It leads to unnecessary hatred and violence. We need only to turn on the news to see the horrific impact it makes. Believe me that Satan loves seeing us tear down one another and create division.

When we are disrespectful or cruel with our words, we imbue another with a sinister and destructive self-perception. We are reminded in the Old Testament that spoken words are extremely impactful: "Kind words are like honey—sweet to the soul and healthy for the body" (Prov. 16:24). When we are gracious with our words, we have the opportunity to be light and hope to a world of hurting people.

Do you remember how it felt the last time you were on the receiving end of ridicule? Can you recall the hurt, the pain, and the helplessness as someone judged or was unkind to you for no apparent reason other than how you looked, dressed, or spoke? Do the feelings recur now as you look back on the incident?

I wish I could say that I have never been unkind to anyone, but that isn't the case. I was the target of ridicule in junior high and high school. Despite understanding the pain and hurt these attacks could cause, upon entering college and developing a new group of friends, I fell prey to the temptation to ridicule others who were different from me. One person in particular—we will call her Liz—was the focus of the unwarranted assaults. Though these typically occurred behind her back, Liz knew that she was being talked about, not being included in group meals, and being purposely left out of social activities.

One night Liz very frankly asked the group why she was being targeted, and we had no valid reason. She hadn't hurt or offended anyone. She was not one to start a negative conversation about someone else. Liz was merely different from us in her appearance, upbringing, and goals. The agony in her eyes still haunts me at times today, decades later, as I know that I was a significant contributor to her pain.

But Jesus teaches a better way. He teaches love, acceptance, and kindness. The golden rule is "Do unto others as you would have them do unto you." What a great rule to live by! Titus, a born-again Christian in the New Testament who has studied under Paul, further encourages us not only to avoid slander but also to show true humility to everyone (Titus 3:2). That *everyone* includes the person toward whom we may have just been unkind. It includes all humankind because we are all God's children.

Put yourself into the shoes of the one you are currently tempted to criticize. Take a moment to truly visualize how you would feel if someone were to treat you that way. Understand the negative impact your words or actions may have if you follow through. Now close your eyes and see that person as the beloved child of God that they are. Allow that truth to penetrate your thoughts and your heart. Then use the power of the Holy Spirit in you to make a different choice. Listen to Jesus as he teaches us to build up one another.

I wish I could go back and choose a different path with Liz, but it is too late for that. I wish I could treat her the way I wanted to be treated. I wish I had seen her as the loved child of our heavenly Father that she was and is. I wish I had chosen kindness, compassion, and unconditional acceptance.

It is not too late for you though. Fight the temptation to live by social comparisons that do not benefit you or others. Everyone feels beaten by the circumstances of life at times. Rather than feeding those insecurities and tearing down other people, you can provide healing by making a positive difference in someone's life. Offer support and reassurance to other people. It is a mutually beneficial way to feel worthy and promote positive emotional growth. It also creates an encouraging example for others to follow.

Remember that we are all designed in God's image, and we are all created with an innate desire to feel accepted and loved. Envision being the vessel that overflows with goodness toward others with words of encouragement, kindness, and hope. Imagine the joy in being a positive catalyst to someone else's sense of worth, setting free their bottled-up hopes and dreams.

Allow the Holy Spirit to ignite within you, friend, the desire to bring care and empathy to a hurting world. When you choose to speak words of kindness and acceptance as modeled by Jesus, the flame of compassion kindles within your soul. You can then spark a transformation in others as they witness your kindheartedness. Become the positive change that you want to see in the world.

VERSES TO ENCOURAGE YOU

So, now I am giving you a new commandment: Love each other. Just as I have loved you, you should love each other.

—John 13:34

Since God chose you to be the holy people he loves, you must clothe yourselves with tenderhearted mercy, kindness, humility, gentleness and patience. Make allowance for each other's faults, and forgive anyone who offends you.

—Colossians 3:12–13

And I will give you a new heart, and I will put a new spirit in you. I will take out your stony, stubborn heart and give you a tender, responsive heart.

—Ezekiel 36:26

Love each other with genuine affection, and take delight in honoring each other.

—Romans 12:10

SONGS FOR YOUR SOUL

- "Speak Life" by TobyMac
- "King of My Heart" by Kutless

A CONVERSATION WITH GOD

Gracious God,

This world can be so cruel at times. By speaking unkind words, I am only contributing to an epidemic of hatred. I want to be different, Father. I want to love the way Jesus has taught us to love. Help me build people up rather than tear them down. Give me your wisdom to see when I am headed down a path of unkindness and fill me with your Holy Spirit to change my thoughts. May my words be a vessel of encouragement and hope. Amen.

NOTES

CHAPTER 8

When Things or Money Become Too Important

Beware! Guard against every kind of greed. Life is not measured by how much you own.

—LUKE 12:15

We live in a materialistic world. The American dream tells us that if we work really hard, we can achieve and get anything we want. So we keep doing more and more to try to acquire more and more. The problem is that *more* is never enough. Social psychologist Erich Fromm speaks of the futility in materialism: "Greed is a bottomless pit which [*sic*] exhausts the person in an endless effort to satisfy the need without ever reaching satisfaction."

Are you feeling exhausted by the constant striving to have enough? Do you find yourself comparing your clothes or home or car or vacation budget with others? This striving robs us of our current joy and can lead to never feeling good enough, fulfilled, or worthy. But, friend, you *are* worthy, just as you are with whatever you have. The New Testament book of Luke cautions, "Beware! Guard against every kind of greed. Life is not measured by how much you own" (Luke 12:15).

Not only may we never feel fulfilled but this desire for material wealth also can lead to workaholic tendencies, self-absorption, disregard for others, and greediness. Some go to the extent of cheating, lying, or stealing to obtain something that they want, believing they deserve it. Can we rationalize these choices? Can we explain away crushing someone else's goals or spirit to get what we want? Is having an abundance of wealth or material things worth whatever it takes to get there?

Let's be clear: having wealth is not in and of itself evil. It allows us to become independent, meet our physical needs, enjoy certain opportunities, and prepare for the future. It also provides the means to be generous to others who may be less fortunate. The difficulty begins when the desire to have more wealth controls all our behaviors. Rather than using our accumulated funds for good, greed leads to a heart of stone toward others. The problem is when we take a potentially good thing, money, and make it a god in our lives, no matter the cost.

Greed is defined as an intense and selfish desire for something, especially wealth or control. It is a condition of the heart that indicates we value possessions and power above people. This egocentric pursuit creates such a disconnect that we often don't recognize the ramifications of our behaviors. The hunger for money can have detrimental effects physically, socially, and spiritually—such as anxiety, sleepless nights, unhappiness, loss of relationships, and separation from God.

The New Testament shows a different way. The first-century Macedonian churches were experiencing poverty and affliction as they were persecuted for their Christian faith. Despite financial hardships, they gave generously from what little they had to meet the needs of others. Their joy in the Lord and overflowing love for others helped them see beyond their present wants and needs.

> They are being tested by many troubles, and they are very poor. But they are also filled with abundant joy, which has overflowed in rich generosity. For I can testify that they gave not only what they could afford, but far more. And they did it of their own free will. They begged us again and again for the privilege of sharing in the gift for the believers in Jerusalem. (2 Cor. 8:2–4)

God teaches us to love people rather than things. He does not judge us worthy based on the number of goods, assets, or properties we are able to buy or accumulate in a lifetime. He instead teaches charity and generosity, helping others using our plentiful resources. He shows the way of responding to a need rather than living a life of greed. As we shift our focus from self to others, God responds by providing for us generously as well. We can never outgive God.

Consider the effect of seeing a person with a specific hardship, one that we can help relieve because of our financial situation. We can pretend we don't notice, look the other way, or rationalize that we aren't able to help. It doesn't affect us after all. Or does it? May we feel guilty? May we later wonder what has happened to that person? May we remorsefully revisit them in our mind? What if we learn that tragedy has befallen them, a tragedy we may have been able to help prevent?

Now consider the opposite. What if we reach out to offer assistance? What if we see a need and respond? What if we put someone else's necessities above our own desires? What if we are generous? Generosity has been shown to reduce stress, improve cardiac health, fight depression, enhance a sense of purpose, improve relationships, and increase one's life span.[1] Although we are giving for the good of others, the result is positive for us as well. By focusing outward, we develop more confidence, have fewer selfish tendencies, and can build better and more meaningful relationships.

As we strive to become more like Jesus, we are led down a path of selfless love for others. When someone is truly in need and we reach out with a word of hope, a loving hand, or financial support to get them through their hardship, we bring the kingdom of God to the earth. He wants us to be generous with one another rather than hoard meaningless things. The saying "You can't take it with you" reminds us that when we die, all the things we have accumulated stay right here. The kindnesses we share, however, continue to multiply.

What we do take with us when we die is the love of others and the joy of our heavenly Father, who smiles when we have lived our lives for the right reasons and with the right goals. He is filled with joy when we share with others the resources he has generously provided to us.

So when society seems to push us to selfishness or greed, we need to step back and reflect on who we want to be. What legacy do we want to leave? Our actions in these challenging moments define our character.

Take some time right now to process, meditate, and pray over the items you desire and your current financial situation. It may be surprising and humbling to acknowledge the reality of your abundance. Recognize the blessings you currently have and give thanks to our generous, heavenly Father. Truly distinguish between your personal wants and your basic needs. Are there wish-list items you can cross off?

Chasing after material desires obscures our perspective to the plights of others. It distances us from others and from God. Consider instead sharing with what you have been blessed. Have you recently seen someone in need? What gift of time, monetary contribution, or personal talent can you provide to someone else this week? Visualize being a pitcher of hope-filled water as you pour yourself into a dry, parched, and hurting world. Envision the reality of the positive impact you will have when intentionally keeping a keen eye open and responding to the needs of others. Friend, I lovingly encourage you to live a life of healthy generosity and see how our wondrous God responds. You can never outgive his generosity, love, and grace.

VERSES TO ENCOURAGE YOU

> Be generous: Invest in acts of charity. Charity yields high returns. Don't hoard your goods; spread them around. Be a blessing to others. This could be your last night.
> —Ecclesiastes 11:1–2 (MSG)

> But the one who plants generously will get a generous crop. You must each decide in your heart how much to give. And don't give reluctantly or in response to pressure. "For God loves a person who gives cheerfully."
> —2 Corinthians 9:6–7

Keep your lives free from the love of money, and be content with what you have.

—Hebrews 13:5 (NIV)

Prefer my life disciplines over chasing after money, and God-knowledge over a lucrative career. For wisdom is better than all the trappings of wealth; nothing you could wish for holds a candle to her.

—Proverbs 22:1 (MSG)

SONGS FOR YOUR SOUL

- "American Dream" by Casting Crowns
- "Lose My Soul" by TobyMac

A CONVERSATION WITH GOD

Dear God,

It can be so difficult to see others with things I want and not fall into the trap of wanting them too or working longer hours to accumulate more possessions. During the moments when I see someone else's need, remind me that the best things in life aren't things. Help me see and understand the hardships of the hurting people around me and recognize how I can be generous with what I do have. Help me spend time building relationships with others rather than accumulating possessions, living into the generosity you desire of me. In Jesus's name, I pray. Amen.

NOTES

CHAPTER 9

When You Need Encouragement

Strength! Courage! Don't be timid; don't get discouraged.
God, your God, is with you every step you take.
—JOSHUA 1:9 (MSG)

Have you ever diligently followed a sports team? They experience ups and downs with good games and bad ones. Despite the wide variety of talent, almost every team loses at some point. At times, however, a team can get into a rut and keep losing over and over again. Sometimes it becomes hard for the players mentally to get back into the game because they feel defeated.

That's where the coaches, cheerleaders, and fans come in. Shouting words of encouragement, these supporters work to bolster the team's self-esteem and help them refocus on the game. True fans cheer when the team is ahead and when they are losing. But it is when the games are not going well that the players most need to hear that someone still believes in them. They need encouragement to believe that they can win by the final buzzer.

Are you feeling discouraged right now? Do you feel, perhaps like that losing team, that you have fallen into a pattern of repeated failures? Are you overwhelmed? Have you had a string of disappointments that have taken a toll on your overall perspective? If any of this resonates, then you are in good company. We all experience times in life when we need encouragement.

In the Old Testament, Moses leads the Israelites out of captivity and through many trials. But when he dies, his successor, Joshua, feels ill equipped and unprepared to lead the people the rest of the way into the Promised Land. God reassures Joshua that he is not facing the challenge alone: "Strength! Courage! Don't be timid; don't get discouraged. God, your God, is with you every step you take" (Josh. 1:9, MSG). And God reassures that he is also with *you* in each step of your journey.

Author Rick Warren suggests that our discouragement arises from fatigue, frustration, fear, and failure.[1] He offers practical suggestions to decrease the likelihood that this opportunistic barrier will take hold of us. First, get plenty of rest. Our rushed and tired brains are more susceptible to self-doubt and negative self-talk. When exhausted, we tend to make poorer decisions, doubt our value, and give in to the lies and ploys of our spiritual enemy.

Second, frustration can set in when tasks are unexpectedly interrupted or when there is a lack of motivation. When this occurs, we need to try a new method. Keeping our minds open to the possibility that our usual approach may not be the best provides the opportunity to move past the roadblock. We must purposefully look at the situation with fresh eyes and a new perspective.

When fear starts to creep in, we need to remember that fear is not of God. The enemy wants us to be filled with uncertainty and fear of the unknown. Truly trust that God is always in control. When struggling, we must surrender to him and pray for the Lord to give us a brighter view of the situation. And as we rest assured in the confidence that he has the power to do all things, we allow him to provide new energy and a positive outlook.

Finally, we can't allow current or past failures to rule our thoughts. Mistakes and perceived failures are often the best way to learn. Former president of South Africa Nelson Mandela spoke of hope during failed attempts: "Do not judge me by my successes; judge me by how many times I fell down and got back up again." We need to get back up, realizing that the knowledge gained from stumbles and missteps helps create a new and wiser path forward.

We are reminded throughout the Bible that difficult circumstances and challenging seasons bring an opportunity to trust in and rely on God. He promises that he will give us strength (Ps. 28:7), that he will bless our godly efforts (Ps. 37:5), and that when we persevere, our determination will be rewarded (2 Chron. 15:7). And in Matthew 19, we are reminded that *all* things are possible with God. So don't lose hope and don't give up.

Do you have people in your life who can support and cheer you on to victory—victory in your struggles, your work, your relationships, your doubts, and your journey with Christ? We all need someone to reach out to when we are feeling discouraged, unsure, or defeated. We need an earthly advocate who can speak louder than our boisterous inner critic. God places specific people in our lives to do just that—support and lift us when we are feeling down and out.

Take a moment to reflect on whom you can trust with your fears, failures, and dreams. While you're feeling low, now may be a good time to call or text that person and set up a time that you can connect. They may be the exact beacon of hope you need today. If no one comes to mind, I lovingly encourage you to begin prayerfully processing who in your life may be able to fulfill that role. Then take a risk and reach out to that person.

Do you also realize that we all have our own coach, cheerleader, and fan? Life is not a game, but we all experience many joys, challenges, and perceived failures. When having good days, it's easy to sail on through without much thought or extra effort. It's during those bad days or seasons when nothing seems to be going right that we can easily become discouraged. These times make us most vulnerable to self-doubt and self-defeat.

It is during these stretches that we need to remember the availability of our holy personal team. The Holy Spirit is your sagacious coach and will provide needed wisdom during challenges. Jesus is your cheerleader, walking right beside you and urging you forward. He will even carry you if needed, gently reassuring you through the fatigue, frustration, fear, and failure. Listen for Jesus cheering you onward despite feeling discouraged.

God is our number-one fan and will never give up on us. He is supporting us through all of life's hills and valleys. As Creator, God knows what wonderful things we are capable of accomplishing, and he wants each of us to know and believe it too. He will pursue us when he senses us drifting away from him, the Source of all hope. Our Father is always encouraging us to get back on our feet, to keep our head high, and to push onward. As former US president Ronald Reagan said, "We are never defeated unless we give up on God."

Friend, don't wait until you wallow in the pit of your perceived failures before listening for God. Know that he is a loving and faithful Encourager and Redeemer, always walking right beside you in life's joys and challenges. Allowing him to share in your successes by giving thanks in the good times makes it easier to remember to turn to him when you are feeling defeated. The wonderful truth is that you are believed in and loved when winning *and* when losing. He and the rest of your personal team are cheering for you to persist in faith and know you can triumph in the end.

Keep your heart and mind open to hearing the wise counsel of the Holy Spirit. Acknowledge and lean into the gentle persistence that Jesus provides. And listen for your number one fan, cheering to help carry you through the battles and sail atop the clouds in your victories. When open to hearing your holy personal team of encouragers, you have the power to succeed. That is how, despite everything else, you can rise above the circumstances of life and be victorious. You've got this!

VERSES TO ENCOURAGE YOU

God has said, "Never will I leave you; never will I forsake you."
—Hebrews 13:5

Commit everything you do to the Lord. Trust him, and he will help you.
—Psalm 37:5

Jesus looked at them intently and said, "Humanly speaking, it is impossible. But with God everything is possible."

—Matthew 19:26

When doubts filled my mind, your comfort gave me renewed hope and cheer.

—Psalm 94:19

SONGS FOR YOUR SOUL

- "You Say" by Lauren Daigle
- "By Faith" by 7eventh Time Down
- "Fighting for Me" by Riley Clemmons

A CONVERSATION WITH GOD

Dear God,

I feel frustrated at times, not sure that I can live up to the expectations of others or even those I have for myself. I am losing energy and faith. Put in my heart the name of someone who can be my encourager during these times and give me the bravery to reach out. Help me understand that, even if I fail in my eyes or the opinion of someone else, you will never give up on me. Help me lean into the truth that you love me for who I am and not what I do. Thank you that I am still your beloved child, mistakes and all. Amen.

NOTES

CHAPTER 10

When People Are Hurtful

They have greatly oppressed me from my youth, but they
have not gained victory over me.

—PSALM 129:2

Why are people so mean? What
drives someone to attack, be rude,
intimidate, criticize, or put down other people? Today we deal with not
only verbal and physical abuse but cyberbullying as well. It is quite easy
for people to spew malicious messages via text or the internet when they
don't have to see the victim's actual response. It's almost as if there aren't
any repercussions for the ruthless behavior.

Bullying isn't limited to the internet and doesn't only occur among
the youth. We may be the target of these intimidations at various times
throughout life. And unfortunately, the effects of these attacks can be
devastating. Actor Michael J. Fox, after developing Parkinson's disease
at a young age, stated, "One's dignity may be assaulted, vandalized, and
cruelly mocked, but it can never be taken away unless it is surrendered."
We need never surrender our dignity or self-worth.

Despite the wounds of rejection or verbal assaults that you are
currently nursing, know that you are worthy of love. The majestic
Creator of the universe is also your personal healer. Don't be afraid to
give voice to the reality of your pain by crying out to God in anguish

and frustration as he massages a restorative salve on your abrasions. He holds you and this moment in his powerful presence and is eager to begin your healing.

King David faces many bullies and enemies in the Old Testament. Despite the long line of tormentors casting taunts and threats, he recognizes the protection that God has provided throughout his life: "They have greatly oppressed me from my youth, but they have not gained victory over me" (Ps. 129:2). David sees the gracious hand of his sovereign protector repeatedly shielding him from harm. And David's awareness of God's provision and shelter gives him courage to continue moving forward despite naysayers.

Most of us have likely been the victim of these types of assaults and can attest to the pain they cause. Studies by Danish researchers Åse Marie Hansen, Annie Hogh, and others confirm that there is a physiological stress response to bullying. We experience decreased morning cortisol levels, which can lead to discouragement, depression, anxiety, and withdrawal.[1, 2] So can an intellectual response to bullying have a positive effect both mentally and physically?

The answer is yes! We must begin by understanding that cruel behavior toward us is more about the tormentor than about us. Engaging in harassment and intimidation are often signs of low self-esteem. The bully may be hurting emotionally, and belittling someone else allows them to feel better about themselves. Or they may be experiencing verbal or physical abuse at home, and lashing out at others helps them feel that they haven't completely lost control. By recognizing the possible root of the unkind behavior, we can try to lessen the negative impact by taking the attacks less personally.

Having been victim of these types of attacks both as a youth and an adult, I continue to learn to deal with the situations and grow from them. When I was a teenager, a trusted friend would intentionally leave me out of group activities and then brag about how much fun the rest of the group had the next time we were all together. It was hurtful at a time in my life when I was trying to establish my identity and find acceptance.

Later in life, a colleague I had financially supported and mentored for years felt it important to point out their perceived shortcomings of me instead of thanking me for my generosity, time, and grace through their early years of learning and practicing the nuances in the field. Confirmation from numerous other trusted sources that these alleged weaknesses were decidedly inaccurate helped me understand that the person was likely battling personal pain. When burdened by our own wounds and insecurities, we often fail to see the resultant skewing of our perspective. Encouragement from colleagues, family, and friends, as well as reassurances from a tenderhearted God, helped heal my personal wounds of rejection.

I would have loved to tell you that I immediately handled these situations perfectly, but that was not the case. Feeling hurt and confused, I gave in to the ever-present temptation to complain and even gossip. It took time (years), an abundance of intentional self-reflection, and a compassionate search to understand others to be able to grow in a positive way through these experiences.

Do you have similar stories? Most of us do. Suffering through these types of rejections is difficult. The subsequent hesitancy to trust others can lead to building barriers of self-protection that inhibit our ability to engage in meaningful relationships. As one on the other side of many such offenses, I believe overcoming them makes us stronger. So how do we best respond when experiencing these kinds of attacks? How can we move past them without allowing the pain to affect us too deeply and giving in to the temptation for retaliation?

In her article "Why Are People Mean? Don't Take It Personally!"[3] Dr. Monica Frank suggests several reasons for meanness. These include a lack of awareness, miscommunication, misdirected intentions, feelings of superiority, attempts to control others, and self-protection. She reports a variety of low-self-esteem defense mechanisms that lead to bullying. While being able to identify these defense mechanisms doesn't excuse them, it can help us better understand the perpetrator, have compassion, and ultimately forgive.

Self-protection subconsciously leads people to behave in ways that may be outside their true character. By desperately attempting to guard themselves, regardless of whom they hurt or the consequences, these people can show severe malice. They are often trying to compensate for a self-deficiency, prior mistakes, or an unwillingness to accept responsibility. In fact, many tend to call out the faults in others that they don't like in themselves. While some may recognize the error of their ways and apologize, others lack the self-awareness to comprehend the cause for the behavior and think it is acceptable.

When suffering from low self-esteem, people use a variety of defense mechanisms to cope and feel superior. In projection, instead of admitting personal shortcomings, the offender accuses someone else of the behavior they won't acknowledge in themselves. Jealousy can also lead to malice: the intimidator criticizes others to feel better about themselves. Understanding these possible explanations for the bullying behavior can help a victim control their response.

In the Sermon on the Mount, Jesus walks us through how we should respond when people assault or insult us (Matt. 5:38–48). If someone strikes, don't hit back. If someone takes advantage of us, respond with kindness and generosity. If someone gossips about us, pray for them. Jesus expresses that it is easy to love our friends and those who are lovable, but it is in how we respond to those who treat us poorly that our heart intentions are seen. In walking through our spiritual journey with Christ, the true testament of growth and maturity is shown in the way we treat our enemies.

Although the instinct may be to fight back, stoop to their level, or talk about their unkindness with other people, the most effective response is compassion. Now I *know* this is not easy. But where there is cruelty, there is pain, both in the one doling it out and in the one receiving it. Retaliation leads to more pain, opens the door for the enemy to harden our hearts, and ultimately is often a source of deep regret.

Accept and work through your pain first. It is important to acknowledge, at least to yourself, that you have been wounded. Accept that you are not responsible for other people's malicious words or actions. Then attempt to understand the underlying source of their pain. Try to view them with an empathetically open mind and heart, knowing that they also are broken and feel threatened by you in some way. Pray that the source of their pain and self-doubt be healed. Praying in a positive way for those who have caused us harm opens the door to God's generous healing in our own injured hearts.

Putting these methods into practice takes intentionality, time, and energy. As challenging as it is, I encourage you to pray right now for the person who has hurt you. Take some cleansing breaths to breathe out negativity and allow the Holy Spirit to fill your heart and calm your mind. When you pray for those who hurt you, rising above the suffering becomes possible. Only then can you regain your true self through the power of the love of Jesus Christ. God's authority alone can heal your gaping wounds. And, friend, he wants you to feel whole, worthy, and loved.

Tapping into the unconditional love that our heavenly Father provides makes it easier to move on from offenses and begin the healing process. You are God's chosen child, beautifully and wonderfully made. He is keeping you afloat while sailing with you in the pursuit of dignity and self-respect over this current sea of pain. Don't let anyone throw shade on that bright and wonderful truth. Seek his face always—his face of love, compassion, and acceptance. In the end, God's approval is the only one that truly matters.

VERSES TO ENCOURAGE YOU

But you belong to God, my dear children. You have already won a victory over those people, because the Spirit who lives in you is greater than the spirit who lives in the world.

—1 John 4:4

Don't ever say, "I'll get you for that!" Wait for God; he'll settle the score.

—Proverbs 20:22 (MSG)

But I say, love your enemies! Pray for those who persecute you! In that way, you will be acting as true children of your Father in heaven. If you are kind only to your friends, how are you different from everyone else?

—Matthew 5:44–47

My eyes grow weak with sorrow; they fail because of all my foes. Away from me, all you who do evil, for the Lord has heard my weeping. The Lord has heard my cry for mercy; the Lord accepts my prayer.

—Psalm 6:7–9

SONGS FOR YOUR SOUL

- "Before the Morning" by Josh Wilson
- "Even When It Hurts" by Hillsong United
- "Jesus, Hold Me Now" by Casting Crowns

A CONVERSATION WITH GOD

Dear God,

This hurts. While I know that I am loved by you and blessed with the exact gifts you want me to have, people's actions shake my confidence. As I am feeling angry, hurt, uncertain, and tempted to strike back, help me seek your face instead of lashing out. Show me the source of pain in my offender so that I may gain understanding and try to offer compassion. When people see me, I want them to also see you, God. Give me the courage to persevere, show kindness to my enemies, and grow stronger through this situation. Help me be more like Jesus. Amen.

 N O T E S

CHAPTER 11

When You Need to Be Brave

So, be strong and courageous! Do not be afraid, and do not panic before them. For the Lord your God will personally go ahead of you. He will neither fail you nor abandon you.
—DEUTERONOMY 31:6

*B*rave can be an intimidating word. A lot of us don't feel courageous, even though the reality of our lives may tell us differently. Is God calling you to be brave right now? Is it time to make a change? Do you need to stand up for something or someone? Are you battling an illness? Do you need to escape an abusive or dangerous situation? Do you want to take a road less traveled or step into an unknown? Do you have a dream to chase? What is keeping you from moving forward?

Fear is usually what prevents us from doing something brave. We battle the what-ifs in our minds and sometimes allow them to paralyze us. Rather than dealing with any of those possible scenarios, we just continue along our current safe path. We choose to remain tucked deeply under our warm security blanket of the known rather than venturing out, subjecting ourselves to the potentially cold and sometimes cruel world of possibilities that awaits us. Yet we are also neglecting the very real opportunity for the warm glow of success. In doing so, we may be losing out on our intended destiny and who God truly wants us to be.

Can you name the specific fear that's causing you to hesitate? By defining the fear, you will be better able to acknowledge and move past it. Is it fear of failure, of what people will say, of being outside your comfort zone, or of losing control? These smothering worries may be keeping you from morphing into the best version of yourself. According to author Margie Warrell in her book *Brave: 50 Everyday Acts of Courage to Thrive in Work, Love, and Life,* "Daring to expose yourself to those monsters in your head is ultimately far less frightening than spending your entire life running from them."[1]

Despite your hesitations and negative self-talk, there is a world of possibility lying beyond the perceived monsters in your path. You, my friend, are braver than you may think or imagine. God is keenly aware of your full potential that is being smothered under that security blanket. He longs for his children to step out in faith and wants to see all of us succeed in our godly endeavors. So now is the time to face those naysaying monsters head-on.

In the Old Testament, Moses, who had led the people of Israel out of slavery and toward their Promised Land, realized that he would not be able to continue the journey with them. As the Israelites expressed their trepidation in him not seeing them to their intended destination, Moses reassured them, "So, be strong and courageous! Do not be afraid, and do not panic before them. For the Lord your God will personally go ahead of you. He will neither fail you nor abandon you" (Deut. 31:6). Moses wanted the people to remember that our omnipresent God was near to them in each of their life challenges. And he is always there for you too.

Each moment in our lives helps prepare us for the next. We crawl before we toddle, toddle before we walk, and walk before we run. The skills and strength learned in each step help prepare us for the following part of our journeys. Being courageous works the same way. Taking a small step out of our comfort zones prepares us to face the next bigger challenge. And with God's grace, we can continue to courageously move beyond our self-perceived and self-imposed limitations.

In 1 Samuel 17:37, we learn that David killed a lion and a bear before having the courage to stand up to Goliath: "The Lord who rescued me from the paw of the lion and the paw of the bear will rescue me from the hand of this Philistine." His success in previous trials gave David the confidence to face the giant before him. Trusting that God was with him helped David be brave in those moments.

Who or what is your giant? What seems impossible or insurmountable today? What is your dream, and what brave act do you need to take right now to pursue it? Know that God is with you too, my friend. Think about the trials God has led you through to bring you to this juncture. You need to believe, like David did, that God has prepared you and goes with you as you courageously take that next leap forward.

Let's get practical and begin the process toward being courageous. First, name how you want to be brave; put it in writing. Sometimes just seeing the words in front of your eyes can make it more of a reality. Put this written goal in a visible place so it remains at the forefront of your mind.

Next, define the fear that keeps you from moving forward so you can acknowledge it and push it aside. Pray for your dream and ask God to guide you to be certain you're moving in the direction he desires for your life. If you sense divine peace and confirmation, pray that he gives you the strength and courage to proceed. Then close your eyes and try to visualize what your life will look like in the future if you are brave right now, chasing that dream. Really see it. Use that vision to bolster your confidence.

Now assume a self-assured stance with your feet apart, shoulders back, and chin held high. Take a deep breath. Go ahead, even if this sounds silly. Really tap into your inner strength through the Holy Spirit. Envision succeeding and feel the power increase within you. Remind yourself of the reasons you want to be brave, that you are capable of moving forward, and that God will be with you every step of the way. The final step is often being willing to catapult yourself decidedly into the unknown.

Any skill we learn in life requires repetition to become proficient, and bravery is no different. It means facing down some of our inner demons and monsters to boldly move in a direction that brings uncertainty at first. It means accepting that we can never improve if we aren't willing to change. It means relying on the Lord's strength when the going gets rough, trusting that, even when things are difficult, it can be a positive learning experience.

The plan may not go exactly as you have thought or hoped, but at least you are advancing on that courageous path toward your dream. Can you do it? Of course, you can! Your prior successes and failures have prepared you for this moment. Move forward past the monsters of doubt, remembering that all things are possible with Christ. And each time you venture out from under that cozy security blanket, despite reservations, you weaken the power fear has over you, your choices, and your life. Sometimes the only way to get from where you are to who you want to be is to take a leap of faith. Go ahead, friend. Be brave. Leap now.

VERSES TO ENCOURAGE YOU

Faith is the confidence that what we hope for will actually happen; it gives us assurance about things we cannot see.

—Hebrews 11:1

This is my command—be strong and courageous! Do not be afraid or discouraged. For the Lord your God is with you wherever you go.

—Joshua 1:9

With all of this going for us my dear, dear friends, stand your ground. And don't hold back. Throw yourselves into the work of the Master, confident that nothing you do for him is a waste of time or effort.

—1 Corinthians 15:58 (MSG)

Don't be afraid, for I am with you. Don't be discouraged, for I am your God. I will strengthen you and help you. I will hold you up with My victorious right hand.

—Isaiah 41:10 (NLT)

SONGS FOR YOUR SOUL

- "You Make Me Brave" by Bethel Music
- "Voice of Truth" by Casting Crowns
- "Confidence" by Sanctus Real

A CONVERSATION WITH GOD

Dear God,

I have a dream that requires making a big change, and I am afraid—afraid that I am not making the right choice, that it won't work, or that people will laugh if I fail. I need your wisdom to know if this is the right path for me. And if it is, grant me the courage and strength that only you can provide to step bravely forward in Jesus's name. Amen.

NOTES

CHAPTER 12
When You Need Physical Healing

Jesus turned and saw her. "Take heart, daughter," he said, "your faith has healed you." And the woman was healed at that moment.

—MATTHEW 9:22

A uthor Ernest Hemingway said, "We are strongest in the places we have been broken." When battling an illness or injury, however, it is typical to feel anything but strong. Whether suffering from a mild ailment, an unexpected injury, or a chronic illness, we may feel frightened, frustrated, discouraged, and exhausted. Our strength wanes as the body depletes all energy reserves to allow our immune defenses to promote healing. Optimizing our immune system and returning to health requires abundant self-care, which is often difficult to do in the chaotic rat race of life. We also need to trust that God is with us in our battle for health.

When Jesus walked the earth, he healed hundreds of people of physical, mental, and spiritual ailments. Word spread throughout the region of his miraculous healings. A long-suffering woman who had been bleeding for twelve years ventured to secretly touch Jesus's robe, knowing that would be enough to cure her illness. When he felt power go from him to the woman, "'Take heart, daughter,' he said, 'your faith has healed you.' And the woman was healed at that moment" (Matt. 9:22). His words expressed that she was a daughter of God, and his love for her was displayed through restoring her health.

We, too, can pray to God for comfort and the healing of our ailments. But we also must contribute to the healing process. Rest and nutrition are paramount to the success of the immune system, which is our natural defense mechanism against any type of illness or injury. After detecting a foreign particle in the body, whether in the form of a virus, bacteria, cancer cell, or other material, the immune system kicks into action to try to neutralize that threat. A complex cascade of events occurs that ultimately releases specific chemicals into the bloodstream to combat and hopefully eliminate the culprit. The immune system also greatly affects healing from wounds and injuries through its impact on several repair mechanisms in the body.

The human immune system is a remarkable display of God's incredible workmanship and attention to detail. For instance, when bacteria attacks the body, a response is mounted specific to that illness-causing pathogen. Through a multitude of intricate steps, antibodies (proteins aimed at fighting off the problem) are formed. The resulting antibodies target only that bacteria and no other. Each step in the process is dependent on the phase before it, and subsequent steps cannot occur until the full prior sequence has been completed. Our bodies also create something called memory cells, so the next time our body encounters that form of bacteria, our immune response gets up to speed more quickly to fight off the illness better.

Unfortunately, the body's natural response isn't always enough to completely eliminate the problem, sometimes making the use of medicines and other supportive measures a necessity. Some medications can have undesirable side effects, which leads to an even greater need for rest and self-care. This is especially true for those battling cancer, for treatments can damage healthy cells along with the cancer cells. All this is to emphasize the fact that various sicknesses and injuries take a serious toll on our bodies. So what can we do to help the process, and how does God play a role in our healing?

As already mentioned, one of our responsibilities in the process is to make self-care a priority while fighting any illness. This includes extra sleep, daytime rest, increasing clear fluid intake (no, coffees and sodas don't count), and eating nutritious foods, such as vegetables, fruits, and healthy proteins, to boost our immune system. Smoking,[1] alcohol,[2] and illicit drug use[3] are harmful to the immune system and will substantially prolong the healing process. If the goal is rapid restoration of health and returning to a normal routine, all these should be avoided.

We must also take measures to increase the energy available in our bodies that can be directed toward the healing process. Ask friends or family members to help with the kids. Tell the boss we need a day or two off to begin recovery. Take a daytime nap, even if the to-do list seems to be a mile long. Our body's ability to mount the appropriate and needed immune reaction, as well as the speed with which it can function, is dependent on its strong response, so we need to set ourselves up to use it to its full capacity.

As we do our part, how can we be certain that the Lord is doing his? God assures that he is with us in this battle when, in Isaiah 41, he says, "Don't be afraid, for I am with you. Don't be discouraged, for I am your God. I will strengthen you and help you." In Jeremiah 33:6 (NIV), he promises, "I will heal my people and will let them enjoy abundant peace and security." When we're coping with an injury or illness, God's promise to bring peace and security is like a cold glass of lemonade on a hot summer day. It is refreshing and reenergizing.

And we should never underestimate the power of prayer in recovery. During self-care periods of rest, pray for God to remove any obstacles that may be in the way of healing. Pray for his gentle yet powerful healing touch and for restoration to complete health. Pray for the health-care team that is providing treatment and for the medications to be effective and rapid acting. Pray to have the strength of mind and will to avoid situations that may delay healing and instead to engage in the healthy lifestyle needed to get well. Share health concerns with a trusted friend and ask them to pray too.

There are numerous stories of miraculous healing that can inspire and speak to the power of prayer. Dr. Kent Brantly, a medical doctor who served in Liberia through the charity Samaritan's Purse, was providing care for many months there before the highly infectious Ebola virus made its way into that West African country. Three days after safely evacuating his family, Brantly developed symptoms of the disease, which had a mortality rate of up to 90 percent. He immediately put himself in isolation and was later confirmed through testing to have contracted the dreaded disease that he was selflessly trying to eradicate in others.

Millions of people around the world heard Dr. Brantly's story via news sources as his care moved from Liberia to Emory University Hospital in Atlanta. His prayer was that God be glorified through his life or through his death. As the Ebola virus ravaged his body, thousands upon thousands of people around the globe prayed for his healing. By God's grace, Brantly's life was spared, and after a month of medical isolation, he was able to reunite with his family. Upon his hospital departure, he thanked the many professionals who had provided him care, those who had cared for his family, and the thousands who had prayed for him: "Above all, I am forever thankful to God for sparing my life." After witnessing numerous tragic deaths from Ebola in his own patients, he called it a miraculous day.

Believe that God is in the business of miracles, friend. I don't want to imply your road to recovery will be an easy one. Depending on the severity of the illness or injury, you may be looking at painful weeks, agonizing months, or even seemingly never-ending years to return to a state of full health. I lovingly encourage you to summon all your energy and use this healing process to draw nearer to God. Share your hurt and frustration with him as you pray for recovery. He will absolutely help you carry this heavy burden, ease your mental and physical pain, and tenderly provide you both strength and hope.

Prayer is the best way to draw closer to God. In her memoir *Beauty in the Broken Places*, Allison Pataki describes the agony and triumphs she experienced during her thirty-year-old husband's severe illness and recovery. She recalls a conversation with one of her husband's physicians, Dr. Omar Lateef, early in the journey. The doctor said, "Pray. Pray to whatever deity you believe in, or ask the universe, or meditate—however you think of prayer. I really believe it helps in ways we can't explain."[4] Many physicians have witnessed the power of prayer defying logic and scientific reasoning.

And, friend, sometimes full physical healing doesn't come. Never assume that God has abandoned you or doesn't hear your prayers if that is the case for you. I don't pretend to understand, for example, why some people defeat cancer and others succumb. But I do know that the Lord's abundant love for you transcends all pain, and he is walking with you through this difficult journey. For those who don't experience healing on this side of heaven, he provides an everlasting hope for a painless eternity through his Son, Jesus Christ.

I am so sorry that you are battling a physical challenge right now. I understand the frustration and fear that you may have in looking at the tortuous road ahead. It is OK to feel discouraged and to cry out in frustration. Give yourself permission to grieve the previously healthy body you've had while looking ahead to the best path toward restoration. And it is essential to allow others to help you in this season. Relinquish the self-reliant temptation to be fiercely independent in the process and take comfort that you do not have to travel this journey alone. God, too, is with you. He loves you deeply and wants you to be fully healed.

Today make sure that you are doing your part in pursuing the pathway to restored health. Keep your immune system as healthy as is in your control. Allow others to lovingly provide help and support so you can focus on resting and recuperation. Pray for God to show up in a powerful way in the healing process and to bring you peace of mind and comfort for your weary spirit. Pray that he be glorified through your battle, regardless of the outcome. And trust that while you are doing your part to heal, he, who loves you beyond measure, will *always* do his.

VERSES TO ENCOURAGE YOU

But those who hope in the Lord will renew their strength. They will soar on wings like eagles; they will run and not grow weary, they will walk and not be faint.
—Isaiah 40:31

The Lord nurses them when they are sick and restores them to health.

—Psalm 41:3

I pray that from his glorious, unlimited resources he will empower you with inner strength through his Spirit.

—Ephesians 3:16

I am leaving with you a gift—peace of mind and heart. And the peace I give is a gift the world cannot give. So don't be troubled or afraid.

—John 14:27

SONGS FOR YOUR SOUL

- "Healing Hand of God" by Jeremy Camp
- "In Jesus Name (God of Possible)" by Katy Nichole
- "The Healing" by Blanca and Dante Bowe

A CONVERSATION WITH GOD

Dear God,

I pray for your healing hand to make me well. Have mercy on me through this battle in my earthly body and restore me through your life-giving presence. May I feel your power flow through me, giving me strength and courage to endure and to be restored. Through this illness, may all I say and do glorify only you. In Jesus's name, I pray and trust. Amen.

NOTES

CHAPTER 13

When You Feel Worried

> Don't worry about anything; instead, pray about
> everything. Tell God what you need, and thank Him for
> all He has done. Then you will experience God's peace,
> which exceeds anything we can understand.
> — PHILIPPIANS 4:6-7

Why do we worry? Worry is giving way to anxiety and allowing one's mind to repeatedly dwell on difficulties or troubles. It is as if we somehow believe that if we worry enough about something or someone, we can prevent bad things from happening. Have you ever found this to be true? As I look back on situations where I have given way to worry, I cannot think of even one where it has been constructive.

In Paul's New Testament letter to the church in Philippi, he encourages the people to bring their specific concerns before God: "Don't worry about anything; instead, pray about everything. Tell God what you need, and thank Him for all He has done. Then you will experience God's peace, which exceeds anything we can understand" (Phil. 4:6-7). As we navigate the turbulent waters of a seemingly endless sea of stressors and anxieties, the reassurance of God's peace that surpasses all understanding can bring hope to our overwhelming circumstances.

Whatever situations are currently threatening your peace of mind, take heart in that truth. In surrendering your current troubles to our powerful, kind, and loving God, you will have the opportunity to experience his permeating presence of peace that is beyond human comprehension. Being filled with that stillness brings an abrupt reversal to the destructive spiral of worry to which we often fall prey. It proffers a serene reward to the tormented spirits of those who willingly let go and let God.

Anxiety can be a normal response to stress. It may even keep us alert in important situations, such as an interview or an exam. A small amount of anxiety may be beneficial in encouraging us to be better prepared for a new job, intense case, or upcoming move. Excessive worry, however, has detrimental effects on our bodies and minds. When we continually focus on the potential negatives in a situation, it may start a downward spiral and lead to extreme anxiety. Some people eventually experience panic attacks, which can be severe and debilitating.

Physical symptoms of worry or panic include a racing heart, chest pain, rapid breathing, dizziness or lightheadedness, muscle tension, sleeplessness, nausea, stomach pains, diarrhea, sweating, and dry mouth. Some people become irritable, have difficulty concentrating, and become ineffective in their jobs or other responsibilities as a result. People may experience only a few of these symptoms or many, but either way, in the long run, there are harmful effects on the body and mind. If you are experiencing these types of symptoms, take heart in knowing that you are not alone.

Carried to the extreme, worry or ongoing fear can become so irrational that clear thought processes and reasonable responses are lost. People with this type of high-level anxiety dwell almost exclusively on the negatives, which can lead to depression. It is in the midst of these downward spirals of worry that we need to find a way to halt the ambush of negativity. Leaning on our faith can provide bits of hope.

In the Sermon on the Mount in the book of Matthew (6:25–34), Jesus addresses the topic of worry. He warns the disciples not to be anxious about anything because God will care for all their needs: "Seek the kingdom of God above all else, and live righteously, and he will give you everything you need" (Matt. 6:34). Jesus also encourages his followers not to worry about the future but rather to live in the present, dealing with problems as they arise. As true as his words were then, they are still true today. Knowing worry is counterproductive, however, doesn't necessarily provide the impetus to stop.

What are some methods to move away from worry and anxiety? We can first deal with the bodily effects by seeing our physician to rule out any physical problems that may be causing the symptoms we are experiencing. That step alone often begins to alleviate some concerns. The doctor can also help determine if the anxiety has reached a point of needing an intervention with therapy or medication.

Worry leads to overeating in some people and undereating in others. Both are detrimental and can cause worsening of the somatic manifestations of anxiety. Maintaining a healthy lifestyle with a well-balanced diet and consistent exercise counteracts some of the negative effects of worry. Eating regular meals to prevent hypoglycemia while avoiding processed and high sugar content foods, which can create a sugar high and mimic a panic attack, helps the body maintain a healthy metabolism. During a time of high anxiety, engaging in a physical activity provides an alternate focus that helps ground our mind and allows us to think through the worrisome situation more rationally.

Physical activity also leads to the release of endorphins into the bloodstream. These biochemicals relieve pain, stimulate feelings of pleasure, and help maintain a healthy mind and body. Exercise also helps us be better prepared to handle life stressors.[1] We can continue to care for our body by eliminating or using in moderation both caffeine—which, as a stimulant, can cause symptoms such as rapid heart rate and nervousness—and alcohol, which is a depressant.

After addressing the physical aspects of worrying, it is important to acknowledge the impact it has on our mind. Setting aside a specific time, no more than ten to fifteen minutes each day, to think about our stresses and worries can train our brains to think more positively the rest of the day. We can use that time to recognize whether the worries are unnecessary what-ifs or if they are current real problems we are able to address. The end of the fifteen minutes should be followed by prayer for God to help us release unhealthy worries and find a solution to the problems that require action. Then we need to truly *let go* of the concerns for the rest of the day, not allowing our mind to return to its negative habit. If we find thoughts turning back into worries, we consciously redirect them.

If we continue to struggle with excessive worry, especially if it has given way to physical symptoms, seeking therapy is a viable option. Trained professionals can help us see patterns of thoughts and behaviors that escalate the anxiety that may be overtaking our lives. They can help identify our triggers and provide coping techniques to employ when we start to head into a pattern of worry. Seeking help is not a sign of weakness but rather signifies strength in admitting the problem, a desire to change destructive thought patterns, and courage to begin the healing process.

The Bible tells the remarkable story of Christ walking on water. Jesus has sent his disciples ahead of him to cross the Sea of Galilee. Caught on a boat in the middle of the sea during a nighttime storm with strong winds and waves, the disciples have become anxious and worried. When they alarmingly believe a figure walking on the water toward them to be a ghost, Jesus calls out, reassuring them that it is him and telling them not to be afraid. Peter then says, "'Lord, if it is really you, tell me to come to you, walking on the water.' 'Yes, come,' Jesus said" (Matt. 14:28).

Peter—filled with relief, excitement, and trust in his Teacher—abandons worry and steps out of the boat to find that he *can* walk on the surface of the water. Then he makes an unfortunate error. Looking away from Jesus, Peter again sees the power of the wind and the magnitude of the waves on the sea. Realizing the potential gravity of the situation, Peter begins to sink. After grabbing and rescuing Peter, Jesus admonishes him, "You have so little faith. Why did you doubt me?" (Matt. 14:31).

I love Peter. He is full of passion, excitement, and faith yet has moments of pride, selfishness, and doubt. He makes great decisions at times and fails miserably at others. Much like us, with our successes and failures, Peter is *real*.

The worries and anxieties that we carry are comparable to the winds and the waves that Peter encountered in that tumultuous sea. They are consuming and scary, can disrupt our focus, and can wreak havoc in our minds and spirits. When we fix our eyes on Jesus, however, he provides the ability to move forward atop the sea of our uncertainties. When we fully trust him, even the most worrisome situations become manageable. The problem comes when we look away, allowing the concerns to again take center stage, and begin to sink.

Are you ready to walk above the worry in your mind and reclaim peace? Start by practicing relaxation techniques. Learn to release the toxic stress in your body by concentrating on removing tension from one muscle group at a time, head to toe. Starting at your face, intentionally relax each muscle before moving down to the neck. Slowly and consciously release tightness from each muscle group as you move down the entire body. Take slow, deep breaths and put your mind in a happy place. Try yoga or meditation. And most importantly, open your heart to prayerfully surrendering your stressors to God and keep your eyes fixed on Jesus.

Through prayer, ask the Holy Spirit to give you the courage to relinquish fears and worries to the Lord. There is no question that surrendering anxieties is easier said than done, but it does become less difficult with practice, especially when we trust that Jesus will keep us afloat. Some people find repeating a brief breath prayer, such as "I trust you, God," can help. The physiological response to relaxation techniques is a feeling of warmth and quiet mental alertness. Once you reach this state, you are better prepared for a more productive and less hectic day.

If you are caught up in a chaotic spiral of worry, you are not alone. Most people fall prey to dwelling on difficulties or troubles at various times. I am a frequent victim and can currently name at least three situations that are creating significant worry and angst in my heart and mind. While intellectually understanding this to be an unproductive and dangerous trap, the thought-pattern shift is a serious challenge for me. As hard as I try, there are times I simply cannot let go of the turmoil of worry in my brain. At times, the angst leads to sleepless nights or nauseatingly stressful days. And as I stew and worry, having taken my eyes off Jesus, I finally reach a point of not being able to take it anymore.

Fortunately, we are most likely to invite God to show up in our lives at such moments. He has been standing by patiently, waiting for us to realize that our excessive worrying and anxiety hasn't brought us any closer to resolving the situation. In those moments of accepting our weakness and surrendering our minds to his great power, we create an opening for him to step through to be our Overcomer. Hallelujah that he can and will carry our burdens for us so that we may experience greater peace. We may even sense him saying, "Be still and know that I am God" (Ps. 46:10) as we surrender one concern at a time.

Your heavenly Father wants to rescue you from the exhaustingly detrimental pattern of worry. Don't wait another minute to pray for him to begin to soothe and calmly transform your mind. Friend, it's time to abandon the misguided perception that anything is under your full control. Thank goodness it's not! As fallible humans, we tend to create mental restlessness through our consistent insistence to do things on our own and believe we have it all covered.

Be intentional about keeping your eyes on Jesus and relinquishing to God today at least one worry that is threatening your peace of mind. Once you have released it to him, refuse to look away to the waves and wind or to pick up the burden again. Focus instead on trusting him more and more every day, surrendering each encumbering worry as you are able.

God's calm wisdom and perfect plans are always better than our best attempts at controlling a situation, friend. Believe that generously infinite truth and lean into the God of peace and perfector of our faith. Trust that Jesus truly *will* give you courage to walk above this turbulent sea. Believe in the hope that awaits on the other side. Healing and a peaceful heart are ahead.

VERSES TO ENCOURAGE YOU

Give all your worries and cares to God, for he cares about you.
—1 Peter 5:7

I am leaving you with a gift—peace of mind and heart. And the peace I give is a gift the world cannot give. So, don't be troubled or afraid.
—John 14:27

Don't fret or worry. Instead of worrying, pray. Let petitions and praises shape your worries into prayers, letting God know your concerns. Before you know it, a sense of God's wholeness, everything coming together for good, will come and settle you down. It's wonderful what happens when Christ displaces worry as the center of your life.

—Philippians 4:6–7 (MSG)

Now may the Lord of peace himself give you his peace at all times and in every situation.

—1 Thessalonians 3:16

SONGS FOR YOUR SOUL

- "I Will Fear No More" by the Afters
- "Truth I'm Standing On" by Leanna Crawford
- "The Answer" by Jeremy Camp

A CONVERSATION WITH GOD

Dear God,

I am beside myself with worry. I keep thinking about _____ and can't seem to focus on anything else. It's affecting my relationships and my life in ways I am only beginning to see. I know that following you requires accepting that these situations are beyond my control. I need to rely on you to help me through this, but I'm struggling to let go. Show me the steps I need to take today to work toward peace in the chaos. Help my mind be still and trust in you. Amen.

 NOTES

CHAPTER 14

When You Need to Have More Faith

But when you ask him, be sure that your faith is in God alone.
—JAMES 1:6

W hat does it mean to have faith? A *saving faith* means that someone believes in the person of Jesus, understands what he has done for us through his death and resurrection, and has accepted him into their heart. This is, in essence, believing the Gospel and, therein, the promise of eternal life through Jesus. While this belief is a critical step in becoming a follower of Christ, we often need much more to lean into when experiencing life's struggles.

The Greek word *pistis*, used in the early version of the New Testament to describe another aspect of faith, is expressed as a certainty or guarantee that God exists, is the Creator of all things, and is reliable.[1] In other words, it is the assurance that God is who he says he is and can do what he says he can do. People with this type of faith are convinced that God is real, trustworthy, and good.

Do you truly take God at his word? Have you seen circumstances in your life that confirm his goodness? In a world full of tasks, temptations, and turmoil, we often overlook the small ways in which our heavenly Father is gently loving us and helping lessen the load of our burdens. In the New Testament, James guides the early Christians in how to pray to the Lord: "But when you ask him, be sure that your faith is in God alone" (James 1:6). So how can we become more tuned in to our faithful God, more believing, and more trusting?

The Bible is filled with stories of champions of faith—people who trusted in God when the odds were against them, people who went through deep valleys but never lost faith or hope, people who, despite uncertainty in their lives, leaned on God's Word for direction. These are provided as examples for us to learn from and as sources of encouragement when we begin to doubt.

One of my favorite stories is in the book of Daniel (6:1–28). Because King Darius trusted him and made Daniel a supervisor, Daniel became a target of the other officers. Finding no fault in his handling of government affairs, the men chose to attack Daniel for his faith. After coercing the king to sign into law that no one in the kingdom could worship anyone but the king, they found Daniel on his knees, praying, giving thanks to God, and asking for help. Although wanting to protect him, King Darius was forced to follow through with the law and throw Daniel into the lions' den overnight, saying, "May your God, whom you serve so faithfully, rescue you."

After waking and rushing to the lions' den the following morning, King Darius called out to Daniel. Then Daniel replied, "Long live the king! My God sent his angel to shut the lions' mouths so that they would not hurt me, for I have been found innocent in his sight" (Dan. 6:21–22). The overjoyed king was astounded at the faithfulness of God and sent a decree throughout his kingdom that all should honor and trust God. Daniel's faith not only saved his life but also helped others come to faith in God by his example.

While perhaps not as dramatic as in Daniel's story, there are certainly times God has come through for you too. It often takes deep, prayerful reflection to see the work of the Master in your life. In the next day, set aside time to ask the Holy Spirit to reveal examples of how God has moved in your journey. As situations come to your heart and mind, write them down. Then create a time line of all the instances where you can see the mighty hand of God.

Look at the mountaintops—times when you have been successful or felt you are living your best life. Can you see or feel how God may have been guiding you in those victories? Explore the valleys—times of challenge and suffering. Can you appreciate how God may have been providing encouragement and help along that difficult trail? Even glance into the mundane and everyday events. As you reflect on all these moments or seasons, are you able to recognize the hand of God in your joys and in your challenges? Now create a life time line that includes all these instances where God has appeared in gentle or powerful ways.

After completing this exercise several years ago, I was surprised by how many examples of his faithfulness I was able to identify. The first was when, as a ten-year-old child, I prayed for a dog for my birthday. My parents had said no, so I prayed even harder that I could at least have a dog for my birthday party. After all, the other birthday parties I had been to where there was a family dog had been so much fun! And I certainly wanted my party to be fun too. Ah, the prayers of innocent children. "Let the little children come to me and do not hinder them," Jesus said (Matt. 19:14).

Lo and behold, two days before my party, a dirty, matted stray dog appeared out of the blue on our fairly secluded back porch. When we washed the brown, mangy fur, streams of mud melted away, and a precious white poodle emerged. He was sweet, great with kids, and, of course, the hit of my birthday party.

Even though he had no collar, we learned the following week that he was the much-loved pet of someone in a nearby neighborhood. The owners, tearful and grateful at his return, said that in the eight years the poodle had been with them, he had never gone digging. But then suddenly one day, he did, and he showed up blocks away, on my family's back porch.

While we couldn't keep him, that sweet pooch was the undeniable answer to an innocent child's prayer to have a dog for her birthday party. This temporary gift displayed not only God's miraculous faithfulness but also that he cared about even the tiniest details in my life, all the way back to my young childhood years. I recalled this beautiful moment only after praying for evidence of God in my life as an adult and felt he was saying, *See how much I love you?*

How many times have events happened that seem like luck or coincidence? Was it luck that someone was late for work and just missed being in a car accident? Was it coincidence that another happened to be in the right place at the right time to find out about a great job prospect? Or maybe you almost left something at home, only to go back for your coat and see the needed item sitting on the counter? I can recall numerous of these God coincidences, or "God-cidences," and I suspect if you really take time to think, you can too. These authentic displays of God's faithfulness in our life can work to boost our confidence in him.

Faith is one of the spiritual gifts given by the Holy Spirit (Gal. 5:22–23). People blessed with this gift trust that God is sovereign, he is good, and he always wants what is best for them. They are confident they can put the whole of their life into his hands and are not surprised when prayers are answered or miracles occur. Even in trying or chaotic times, they accept that God is in control. Even when something terrible happens, they know that in his divine power and limitless love, he can use it for good in the future.

Whether faith is a natural gift for you or not, we are all able to work on increasing our faith. It is likely that there are areas of your life in which you are reluctant to relinquish control. Some people are willing to surrender their health but not their work life. Some are willing to submit the safety of their children but want to remain in control of their children's choices. Others are willing to surrender their free time by volunteering but won't yield their finances. Are any of these resonating?

Perhaps you need to take a baby step in the right direction. The best way to move toward greater faith is to take a risk, however terrifying that may be, and submit one part of your life fully to God. Trust without reservation that he will work his good as you rely on him. Truly reflect on how God steps into that situation as you turn it completely over to him. Once you have seen that God can be trusted with something small in your life, it becomes easier to trust him with the big things.

Begin now. Choose one area in your life where you want or need to trust God more. Take a risk, prayerfully surrender it, and watch what he will do for you. Resist the all-too-common temptation to grab it back. Ask the Holy Spirit to fill your heart and mind to overflowing with faith in him, his Word, and his promises. Realize that our heavenly Father loves it when one of his children truly desires to know and depend on him more. He wants your whole heart and your full faith. Watch for God to give you proof that he is trustworthy. And listen for him saying, "See how much I love you?"

VERSES TO ENCOURAGE YOU

But the Holy Spirit produces this kind of fruit in our lives: love, joy, peace, patience, kindness, goodness, faithfulness, gentleness and self-control.
—Galatians 5:22–23

And we know that God causes everything to work together for the good of those who love God and are called according to his purpose for them.
—Romans 8:28

Trust in the Lord with all your heart, and lean not on your own understanding; in all your ways acknowledge him, and he will make your paths straight.
—Proverbs 3:5–6 (NIV)

Jesus said, "If? There are no 'ifs' among believers. Anything can happen."
—Mark 9:23 (MSG)

SONGS FOR YOUR SOUL

- "Promises" by Maverick City Music
- "Stand in Faith" by Danny Gokey
- "Through All of It" by Colton Dixon
- "There Was Jesus" by Zach Williams and Dolly Parton

A CONVERSATION WITH GOD

Dear God,

I believe in you, but I am having trouble trusting you with the big aspects of my life. I want to surrender _____ to you right now. This isn't going to be easy for me to do, so I need your strength to follow through. Please give me gentle cues when I try to take it back under my own control and remind me to release it again. Help me feel your peace as I trust and have faith in you. Amen.

NOTES

CHAPTER 15

When You Feel Ashamed

Fear not; you will no longer live in shame. Don't be afraid;
there is no more disgrace in you.

—ISAIAH 54:4

S *hame* can be defined as a feeling of humiliation that arises from the perception of having done something dishonorable, immoral, or improper.[1] It can be triggered by a variety of life events and accompanied by many different emotions. Those who feel ashamed may also experience envy, anger, sadness, anxiety, and loneliness. Shame can lead to self-criticism and low self-esteem. We have likely all experienced situations that create an overwhelming sense of regret and shame. Please know, my friend, that there is hope beyond your current shame.

Suffering from shame can engulf a person's entire thought process and being. It differs from embarrassment, which is a more minor and short-lived emotion stemming from a social faux pas or momentary event. People experiencing shame may feel utterly worthless, completely humiliated, and desperately unclean. The humiliation can lead to depression and even thoughts of self-harm.

While shame may be felt when someone commits a dishonorable act, such as a violent crime, infidelity, or selling drugs, it also may occur as a result of living with a stigmatized mental illness, suffering from homelessness, battling an addiction, being dissatisfied with one's body, or experiencing a trauma. As *New York Times* best-selling author Debbie Ford once pointed out, "An exciting and inspiring future awaits you beyond the noise in your mind, beyond the guilt, doubt, fear, shame, insecurity, and heaviness of the past you carry around." So how can we move beyond the burdensome baggage of our current shame toward a lighter and brighter future?

In the Old Testament book of Isaiah, God reminds the Israelites that they no longer need to live in humiliation, for he is their Redeemer: "Fear not; you will no longer live in shame. Don't be afraid; there is no more disgrace in you" (Isa. 54:4). Yet people have still not grasped the richness of his mercy. God later sends his Son, Jesus, to die on a cross, visibly absolving us of all our sins and shame. Through his brutal death and hopeful resurrection, we are forgiven for all our sins: past, present, and future. And, friend, that fullness of grace and mercy is available for you.

Research shows that people living in shame hide, self-conceal, and often don't allow anyone to see their true selves.[2,3] Keeping feelings inside leads to self-devaluation and creates a tragic cycle of anxiety, depression, and low self-esteem. This, in turn, often leads to vulnerability and isolation as we avoid relationships and community. The Lord has never intended for us to live alone. We need to be around others who can lift and support us in our times of need, stress, or shame. Escaping from the abyss of humiliation begins by reaching out.

In the New Testament book of Romans, we are reminded that anyone who declares Jesus as Lord over their life will never be put to shame (10:11). Our loving God is standing ready to cleanse us from the weight of our wrongdoing as soon as we ask. He already knows the mistakes we have made, so we don't need to fear confessing them. When we humbly come before the heavenly Father with true regret, he can lovingly remind us that Jesus has taken all our sins with him through his death on the cross. Now we need to leave our shame and guilt there as well. Let me repeat that: we need to leave *all* our guilt and shame at the foot of the cross.

I am so sorry you are experiencing the deep pain that shame creates.

Please don't let your current guilt take control of your life nor sabotage God's plans for you. He loves you just as you are: imperfect, scarred, and bruised. And his plans for you venture far beyond the shame you are feeling. It's time to move past the noisy mind and the heaviness of past mistakes. Jesus has died so you don't need to continue to live there. He wants you to live lightly and freely (Matt. 11:28).

Let's look at ways to revive the esteemed and self-respecting person that God fervently wants you to be. What is causing your shame and guilt? You must recognize the culprit and name it before you can take strides to move past it. Hiding from the truth can be devastatingly harmful, creating barriers and walls between you and others. In acknowledging the ways that shame may be shaping your life, you become empowered to break free from the prison of guilt and humiliation.

Pray for God to show you one or more people with whom you can safely share your heart. As hard as it is, boldly reach out to that person *this week* so you can begin to break down the protective walls your guilt-ridden mind has erected. Share your story with that trusted friend. Cry on their shoulder, if need be, to begin to release the feelings of guilt deep within you. If there is no one you trust enough to be vulnerable with, consider seeking out a professional counselor or therapist.

You can also choose to channel your feelings in a way that nourishes you. Find a creative outlet to express your emotions. Write a story or song, putting into words all that you have kept bottled up inside. Paint a piece of art that reflects your emotions. Or journal all the feelings that are deep within, providing an opening for release and relief. Shame loses its power over you as you bring it into the world and shed light on those dark places in your heart and mind.

Begin to see yourself as God sees you: a beautiful, beloved child of the King, worthy of his love and grace. Write a list of positive affirmations and put them in a visible place so that there is a daily reminder of your good qualities. If you have trouble thinking of your positive attributes, ask someone close to you to do it. They can certainly provide an encouraging list of your good qualities. Return to the list any time the spirit-robbing spiral of shame begins setting in.

As a part of your healing, you must also learn to understand and forgive yourself. Remember that Jesus has gone to the cross and suffered an unfathomable death so all your transgressions will be forgiven. Holding on to shame negates the amazing work he has done on your behalf. Instead, place each poor choice, every doubt, any stigma, and all heaviness in your heart and mind at the foot of the cross. Pray for Jesus to help you leave it right there where it belongs.

You may also think about how you will respond to a friend experiencing the guilt and shame that you are feeling. How will you encourage them? How will you show them love and acceptance? How will God want you to respond to them? Now have that same compassionate response toward yourself. Develop positive self-talk that is loving, caring, and compassionate. Believe in yourself. And rest in the assurance that God believes in you too.

Our heavenly Father loves you unconditionally and wants you to learn to love yourself. The way out of shame requires taking a chance. Take a chance on yourself by allowing light into these dark places you would rather keep hidden. Take a chance on a trusted friend to give you the hope and encouragement you need to continue forward. And take a chance on our faithful and merciful God, who loves you immensely and completely just as you are. Shame has no authority over you, friend. God does. Believe that immutable truth. Then take the first step toward healing today, knowing you are absolutely worth it.

VERSES TO ENCOURAGE YOU

So now there is no condemnation for those who belong to Christ Jesus. And because you belong to Him, the power of the life-giving Spirit has freed you.

—Romans 8:1–2

Let us draw near to God with a sincere heart and with the full assurance that faith brings, having our hearts sprinkled to cleanse us from a guilty conscience and having our bodies washed with pure water.

—Hebrews 10:22 (NIV)

This means that anyone who belongs to Christ has become a new person. The old life is gone; a new life has begun!

—2 Corinthians 5:17

But if we are living in the light, as God is in the light, then we have fellowship with each other, and the blood of Jesus, his Son, cleanses us from all sin.

—1 John 1:7

SONGS FOR YOUR SOUL

- "Love Me like I Am" by For King & Country
- "Any More" by CAIN
- "Perfection" by Switch

A CONVERSATION WITH GOD

Dear God,

I am beginning to realize that I have allowed shame to ruin my perspective on life and my relationship with you. I admit that I am ashamed of _____. Please bring the light of Jesus into this darkness and free me of guilt so that I can begin to forgive myself. Only then will I be able to truly experience your full forgiveness, grace, and healing. In Jesus's name, amen.

NOTES

CHAPTER 16

When You Feel Overwhelmed

When I am overwhelmed, you alone know the way I should turn.

—PSALM 142:3

D o you ever wake up in the morning with a huge list of things that needs to be done on your one day off from work? There are bills to pay, appointments to keep, paperwork piles to sift through, errands to run, laundry to wash, groceries to buy, deadlines to meet, and needs of family members demanding attention. The only way to accomplish it all is to piece the day together like a puzzle, putting the exact tasks in precisely the right windows of time to try to get them all done.

But then something unexpected happens. An appliance breaks, a pet gets sick, a friend who needs to vent phones, or the call comes in that your child is ill and needs to be picked up from school. Sometimes multiple disruptions in the morning throw the entire well-thought-out plan off kilter, leaving the increasingly intense thought *How am I ever going to get everything done?* The day feels like chaos in the making, and you are beginning to feel overwhelmed.

Perhaps you're in a chaotic season of life with young kids and feel that, with the house, your job, and your family, you never have everything under control. Or maybe you're a part of the sandwich generation, caring for aging parents who require a lot of attention yet still raising your own children with multiple activities and numerous demands on your time. Maybe you're supporting a friend or family member with mental illness and are left feeling emotionally and physically drained. Or perhaps you love volunteering but realize you are overcommitted and now find it difficult to have time to run the household and nurture your relationship with your spouse. Have any of these struck a chord?

The obstacles you're facing and the pressure, whether internal or external, to complete everything *now* lead to a frenzied existence. Often accompanied by a roller coaster of emotions, the feeling of being overwhelmed is all too common today. In other words, you are in good company, friend. So don't berate yourself for allowing life to become chaotic. Chances are some or many of the current circumstances are beyond your control. Yet there is strength within you to get past this potentially peace-robbing time of life.

King David, the author of most of the Old Testament's psalms, walked through countless challenges during his reign. Yet he always relied on and trusted in God to show him the right way to move and to carry him through: "When I am overwhelmed, you alone know the way I should turn" (Ps. 142:3). Isn't it encouraging to realize that, despite the heavy situations that may leave us paralyzed with uncertainty, God knows the exact order of working through our decisions and to-do lists that will return us to a place of sanity and serenity? We need only reach out to, pray to, and rely on God when we are feeling unable to summit our mountain of circumstances.

The reality of life's demands on our time can trigger the fight-or-flight response. In fighting, we try to push through, do it all, and refuse to make time concessions. By putting unrealistic expectations on ourselves, we become vulnerable to detrimental effects on our physical and emotional health. This reaction can leave us feeling frenzied, exhausted, overwhelmed, and helpless.

When the flight response kicks in, we become frozen, feeling unable to accomplish anything due to the stress of the mounting time burdens. Rather than begin even one of the needed tasks, we find something, *anything*, else to do. We may escape by surfing social media, playing games on our phone, or binge-watching Netflix. As we do anything *other* than attack the to-do list, our burdens mount, and the feeling of being overwhelmed intensifies.

The latter response can lead to learned helplessness, which "occurs when an individual continuously faces a negative, uncontrollable situation and stops trying to change their circumstances, even when they have the ability to do so."[1] Rather than beginning to work through the list of necessary tasks, we become incapacitated at the thought and do nothing instead. Learned helplessness can stem from low self-esteem and a belief that we can't do anything right. Despite the reality of increased pressure to eventually do the work, the choice to put the task off for now delays the seemingly inevitable outcome of failure. In this all-or-nothing approach, neither extreme is beneficial.

We often are our own worst enemies when it comes to this intense feeling of being inundated beyond our capacities. Putting unrealistic expectations on ourselves, we don't allow for the inevitability of the unexpected. And the ideas of rest and self-care seem to take a back seat to everything and everyone else in our world.

There are physiological consequences to living a harried and rushed life. As we face the overload of daily demands, our bodies sense these as threats and respond by releasing the stress hormones adrenaline and cortisol. Serotonin, on the other hand, which protects against depression and anxiety, plunges. The long-term activation of this stress response system in the body can lead to headaches, difficulty sleeping, problems with concentration, decreased sexual drive, anxiety, depression, weight gain, and heart disease. So how can we break this destructive cycle when life has so many demands?

In her article "The Secret to Managing Being Overwhelmed," Judith Orloff discusses the importance of pacing, a basic energetic rhythm people can be trained to intuitively sense. Pacing allows us to move at a slower but steady rate as we work to accomplish our goals. "Just as heartbeat and respirations tune our physiological tempo, pacing sets our subtle energy clock's timing."[2] Rushing, the opposite of pacing, is quite different from working quickly and efficiently. It creates the feeling of being overwhelmed. In short, rushing leads to the stress response, while pacing brings a more harmonious balance to our life.

The Bible also encourages us to slow down, reminding us that haste leads to mistakes (Prov. 19:2). And more importantly, rushing prevents us from tuning in to God and allowing his peace into our hearts. As our lives become filled with more stress, more responsibility, and more tasks, the tendency is to spend less time in God's Word and in prayer. While building a relationship with Christ may be part of our typical routine or something we want to intentionally pursue, it is often the first thing we let go of when sensing a time crunch. And aren't these the times when we need him most?

The enemy loves when we feel frenzied, stressed, and rushed because it takes away time we can spend on our faith or building relationships. He doesn't want us to reach out to a trusted friend, spouse, coworker, therapist, or God during our times of chaos. No, the enemy much prefers us to believe we are self-sufficient and can handle it all on our own. It is during these times of perceived independence and exhausted striving that we are especially vulnerable to his lies and deceptions.

Sometimes the circumstances of life create unavoidable chaos. Knowing that, we need to intentionally create space in our daily routine for the unexpected. A simple and practical step is to put fewer items on our to-do lists. Don't turn your to-do list into a today list. Begin by choosing only three things to accomplish on a particular day. Knowing that you have six days (keep one day of rest) to accomplish the ten or fifteen items on your list inevitably makes it feel less overwhelming. This method is beneficial both for those who try to do too many things in one day and those who find it hard to begin even one task on the list. Setting the goal at a doable three reduces the pressure and increases self-confidence in seeing the positive results of your efforts.

Schedule breaks in your day and not just meal breaks, taking fifteen minutes for sustenance. Instead, schedule little interruptions during the workday to refocus and regroup. Capture a few minutes to relax and take slow, deep breaths. This allows your mind to refocus, creating increased productivity. Consider a quick power nap if you can manage it. Fifteen minutes of sleep in a busy day can give you a much-needed refresher to allow success. Finally, return to prayer, even if it's just a quick breath prayer, to calm your spirit.

How can you incorporate pacing in your full-speed-ahead life to effect change? Visualize the less-rushed lifestyle you desire. Really see it and work toward capturing that goal. Incorporate a slow, deep, mindful breath pattern to settle your mind, spirit, and body (see appendix). When you sense inner turmoil brewing, intentionally return to the mindful breath pattern, allowing inner peace to wash over you before proceeding. Prayer and meditation are extremely important as you relinquish the perceived need to complete everything today to feel valuable.

Take time to be still with your heavenly Father. It is during those moments of stillness that we become more aware of our need for God and are best prepared to hear his reassurances. Placing times of solitude with him at the top of your priority list honors God and allows him to bring peace to your frenzied soul.

Friend, don't let the enemy win this battle for your heart, mind, and time. Don't believe his lie that asking for help from others or relying on God is a sign of weakness. Instead, take time to be still with God each morning. Many of us have learned that when we do this, the day always goes more smoothly.

Doing less in a day or a week does not make us failures. Despite the internal desire or external pressure to always keep moving and doing, we are not superhumans. We are human beings, not human doings. Humanity requires times of mental, emotional, and physical rest to be our best, most productive, and healthiest selves. Acknowledge this need and afford yourself those times of rejuvenation.

Know you are worthy of God's love just as you are, not based on what you accomplish. Pray for the Lord to guide you in adjusting your schedule and relinquishing your self-imposed demands. Then ask him to provide wisdom in removing any unnecessary items from the to-do list for today, allowing him to carry some of the burdens of your stress. The beautiful part of this process is that, even when you are overwhelmed, God is not. When you're feeling overloaded, give yourself permission to have a day where the only goals are rest, relaxation, and rejuvenation. Creating the space for physical, mental, and psychological respite will benefit both you and those around you.

Incorporating these types of changes requires patience and practice.

It also may mean saying no to things you really want to do. If you feel your identity is built on accomplishments, this can be a tough road to take. But the result of a less rushed and less overwhelmed existence makes it well worth the struggle. When we trust in him, God loves to show up and help us in the small details of life. And it's a great faith builder as you see all he can do.

I believe in you, friend. Lean into your faith. Believe God when he tells you that you are dearly loved for who you are and not all you do. Create space for him in the chaos of feeling overwhelmed by the mountain ahead. Trust in the blessed assurance that if you lay your daily burdens down at the foot of the cross, Jesus will gladly lighten the load as you climb. While unloading the weight of those burdens, allow God's wisdom to guide you on the right path as his peace permeates your body and mind, giving you permission to rest.

VERSES TO ENCOURAGE YOU

Come to me, all you who are weary and carry heavy burdens, and I will give you rest.

—Matthew 11:28

But those who trust in the Lord will find new strength. They will soar high on wings like eagles. They will run and not grow weary. They will walk and not faint.

—Isaiah 40:31

Be still and know that I am God.

—Psalm 46:10

Enthusiasm without knowledge is no good; haste makes mistakes.

—Proverbs 19:2

SONGS FOR YOUR SOUL

- "Another in the Fire" by Hillsong United
- "I Lift My Hands" by Chris Tomlin
- "Honestly, We Just Need Jesus" by Terrian

A CONVERSATION WITH GOD

Dear God,

I am panicking right now with all the demands and pressures in life. As my mind spins to figure out how to keep it all going, I feel like I am drowning in stress. Unfortunately, I am making less time for you just when I need you more. Father, forgive me. Help me focus on you and your Word to show me what is truly necessary for this day. Fill me with your peace in letting go of less important tasks and the stress that comes from trying to drive things that are beyond my control. In Jesus's name, amen.

NOTES

CHAPTER 17

When You Witness an Injustice

God blesses those who hunger and thirst for justice, for
they will be satisfied.

—MATTHEW 5:6

Witnessing unfair treatment of a person or group of people can be disturbing and unnerving. At times, we can't shake the tortured faces and words of the victims. Our heartstrings are tugged so tightly that we may move from discomfort to sadness to internal outrage. What can we do when we recognize an injustice? Can we as individuals really make a difference?

Social activist Mahatma Gandhi said, "To forgive and accept injustice is cowardice." We see injustice and prejudice throughout society as people knowingly or unknowingly discriminate based on, among others, identities such as gender, race, age, sexual orientation, nationality, religion, education, and socioeconomic class. Unfortunately, we see signs of discrimination in children, who learn behavior from trusted grown-ups, and in every decade of adulthood.

We can also see how this type of unfair bias has led to local, national, and global tragedies. It is disturbing and heartbreaking to see or hear about the victims of discrimination in the news. Courage is needed to honestly ask ourselves, "Am I part of the problem, or am I willing to share in the solution?" And if we choose to advocate for the solution, how should we respond when we witness an injustice?

In his Sermon on the Mount, Jesus spoke to the gathered crowds of people in a new and bold way. He described many blessings that awaited those who chose to become disciples. One of the proclamations related to the significance of justness: "God blesses those who hunger and thirst for justice, for they will be satisfied" (Matt. 5:6). Throughout this sermon, sometimes referred to as the beatitudes, Jesus was teaching how humans could begin to bring the beauty and joy of heaven to life on the earth. And with all the issues he could have addressed, Jesus felt it important to encourage justice.

As Christians, we are called to love everyone. Yet is that what people truly see in action? Perceived hypocrisy among Christians has led many to abandon their faith. Are we consistently reflecting the image of our Creator, who has brought each and every human life into being? Or are we seen as judgmental, holier-than-thou contradictions, saying one thing but behaving in a completely different manner? These are tough questions requiring honest self-reflection and prayer.

Christ has spoken of the importance of understanding others, loving everyone, and being peacemakers. As followers of Christ, we have the power of the Holy Spirit within us to promote peace and lead the way to reconciliation and justice as author Latasha Morrison so beautifully outlines in her book *Be the Bridge*,[1] which addresses systemic racism. I believe Jesus will smile as he sees us pouring out his love on *all* others, especially those who are unlike us—those who have been discriminated against, those whom society casts aside. What if the world's primary perception of Christians really is that we *love all others well*?

In the Gospels, we encounter a Jesus who is compassionate, forgiving, peaceful, patient, and unprejudiced and who loves unconditionally. Examples of unfair judgment against others by people in Jesus's time include a crowd wanting to stone a woman caught in adultery, although not the man caught in the same act (John 8:1–11), and a woman seen as a sinner washing Jesus's feet (Luke 7:36–50). How has Jesus responded when faced with these situations?

In the case of the conviction of the adulteress, punishable by death through stoning during that era, we see Jesus take an approach of kindness, patience, nonjudgmental statements, and forgiveness. He calls for anyone who has not sinned to cast the first stone, and the angry mob quietly dissipates one by one. Jesus then lovingly and nonthreateningly encourages the woman to make better choices.

Even though she is a known sinner, looked down on by the religious leaders, Jesus collides with the culture of the day by defending the woman washing his feet. He praises her for the great love she shows him and exclaims her to be saved because of her faith. In both of these cases, Jesus transcends the expectations of those around him by showing compassion, unconditional love, grace, and forgiveness. We also have the opportunity to transcend societal expectations in our response to others.

As I reread and ponder these stories, I find myself wondering, *Are we, as a culture of Jesus followers, living according to his modeled behavior, and am I, as an individual, showing the compassion, unconditional love, grace, and forgiveness that Jesus has shown?* Sadly, I think all too often the answer is no in both cases. The problem arises because loving others well and behaving judgmentally are two mutually exclusive events. We may say we are accepting of all and love everyone, but is that truly what our actions show? And is that truly what God sees in our hearts?

The fact that you are reading this chapter indicates that you have likely witnessed prejudice or injustice in some form. Perhaps a specific issue has been placed on your heart, and you can't seem to shake it. Maybe you've found yourself in tears or have lost sleep thinking about the unfair treatment of another. Once your eyes have been opened to the truth of someone else's painful reality, you just can't unsee it.

What injustice is tugging at your heart today? That plight has been placed there because your heavenly Father knows you can make a difference. You may be thinking, *What can I possibly do to help?* The answer is, "A lot!" The Holy Spirit doesn't move our hearts without full intention and understanding that we can influence the situation. Our purpose becomes evident where our divine gifting and heartfelt passions collide. Trust those nudges and passionately pursue the steps to guide you forward.

Begin by educating yourself about the issue. Understanding the history and depth of the problem, along with any personal or cultural misconceptions, provides a foundation of knowledge to be able to discuss the issue with confidence. Research people or organizations that share a similar passion. Connect with a group of local advocates to learn where they have had successes and where they have run into brick walls. Learning from their missteps can increase your effectiveness in the journey to come.

Think about ways you can use a social media platform to educate about and advocate for justice in this space. Badgering, name-calling, and criticism are ineffective and potentially harmful to any cause. Instead, utilize social media to lovingly encourage and motivate others to positive action, leading the charge with donations of time, energy, and financial resources.

Make it personal. Sit with marginalized people face-to-face, just as Jesus has done. Gently talk with them and get to know their hearts and their hurts. Allow them to openly share their journeys. Be a good listener rather than pouring out personal, political, or historical perspectives. Allow them to be truly seen and heard. Understanding their pain may help further soften your spirit to those who aren't exactly like you.

Bathe your journey to justice in prayer. Turn to scripture and be encouraged by the many passages that address God's passion for kindness. God intentionally places each of us in the right time and position to be able to speak truth and integrity to situations where it is lacking. When facing any type of injustice, we have an opportunity to be a vessel of love, acceptance, and healing. How we respond to someone who is the victim of an unjust act, cultural stigma, or discriminatory bias is a reflection of the light and love Jesus has put in our hearts.

Allow me to share part of my journey to battle a cultural bias in hope that it may encourage you to move forward with yours. My heart is saddened by the apparent exclusivity of many churches when it comes to the LGBTQ+ community. I realize that this statement alone will likely anger, alienate, and frustrate some readers. This is certainly not my intention. God has repeatedly and intentionally placed this issue on my heart for a reason. After years of rationalizing that this is too big of an issue for one person to make an impact, I have eventually decided to trust the promptings of the Holy Spirit. The question has then become, "What am I going to do about it?"

Researching the issue has shown that, according to a recent Gallup poll, the LGBTQ+ component of the population is significantly less religious.[2] Studies and statistics also indicate that 5 percent to 10 percent of our population is gay. The thought of many humans, all created in God's image, not knowing him or even rejecting him has brought me to a place of deep sadness.

As pastor and author Mark Achtemeier asserts in his book *The Bible's Yes to Same-Sex Marriage*, "[I]f an interpretation of biblical law fails to have Jesus as its central reference point, that is a sure sign that we have misunderstood the Bible's teaching." I have begun to understand that when we are not truly loving and wholly accepting of these children of God, we turn our backs on up to one in ten people in our communities. Yet Jesus hasn't turned his back on anyone. In fact, he has made it a point to sit face-to-face with the lost sheep, the people whom others have shunned. Jesus has talked with the marginalized, showing them unconditional love.

In our God-led passion to foster love and acceptance for the LGBTQ+ community, my husband, Jon, and I have studied the Bible and scriptures often referenced in discussions about LGBTQ+ people and the church. We have educated ourselves by reading articles and books on the subject and have met with several pastors who hold various perspectives to gain further understanding. We have observed ardent feelings and beliefs in most people we have encountered.

In the end, we have asked ourselves, *Do our behaviors truly align with Jesus's teaching of loving all? Or are we and others, such as the misguided Pharisees of Jesus's time, missing the heart of God amid our intolerant, black-and-white approach to scripture?* During intense prayer and personal reflection time over this issue, God has taken me to the story of Peter and his visions of the sheet of "unclean" animals coming down from heaven.

In early church times, gentiles were considered outcasts in society. Faithful doctrine and culture of the time dictated that people were not to associate with them nor ever to enter their homes. But after receiving visions from God, the Holy Spirit told Peter to go to the home of a gentile. During his visit, Peter preached to this community, and they received the Holy Spirit. Upon returning to Jerusalem, Peter suffered great criticism from Jewish believers for spending time with those who were considered unclean by society. Peter explained that the Holy Spirit descended onto the gentiles, proving that they were children of God. Through this story, the Lord reminded us that not one of his creations should be considered unclean, and as such, we believe that he has called Jon and me to be accepting, loving, and encouraging to the LGBTQ+ community and their position in God's church (Acts 10:9–28).

In our efforts to obey God's prompting, we continue to sit down with individuals of the LGBTQ+ community and listen to their pain and their journeys. We have learned that while being told they are loved, these children of God often feel anything but loved and accepted in many churches. Their exclusion from certain church activities and volunteer positions, along with the actions of some church members, often leave them feeling judged and rejected. The perceived hypocritical behavior and selective judgmentalism not only alienate the LGBTQ+ population but also affront many millennials and younger generations who advocate so strongly for equality and social justice. Sadly, we have spoken to many nongay people who have also left the church altogether because of their frustration over this issue.

Jon and I try to be positive examples of open hearts and minds. Our hope in bringing this issue to light is to motivate honest personal reflection; to encourage gentle, humble, and open conversations; and to promote peace and loving acceptance. During this journey, we have cried and prayed, become frustrated and tired, and then prayed even more. While we feel some headway has been made, there is much more room for growth, understanding, and softened perspectives. The path of battling this injustice is not an easy one. But as long as we feel God is urging us to continue forward, we won't give up.

Are you ready to fight the injustice that has been weighing on your mind? Do you want to be a source of hope and reconciliation? The steps ahead will likely not be comfortable. Know that only when we step out of the security of our personal comfort zones can God fully utilize us with his power and strength.

Your actions in battling injustice may cause friction among you and fellow followers of Jesus. You can find yourself at odds with friends or family members. Be the light of Jesus in the situation as you gently, lovingly, and humbly explain your perspective. Be certain the enemy will fight you every step of the way. Yet if God has placed this issue on your heart, know that by following his holy nudges, you are working to further his kingdom here on the earth.

As you reach out, don't be discouraged by closed doors and closed minds. Thoughts of *Can I really make a difference since I'm only one person?* may continue to creep into your mind because the enemy loves to create doubt, incite division, and widen the chasm between humans. Know that change is possible, and you can be a beautiful example of, and catalyst for, kindness and inclusivity. Each person, each life, matters. And really *loving well* one, a few, or a group of people who feel rejected or marginalized by society can help bridge the wide divide.

I pray right now over anyone reading this chapter who is feeling moved to battle injustice or discrimination in any form. I pray for your courage and protection. I pray that through pursuing your passion to serve, you will be a humble reflection of our heavenly Father and his unconditional love. I ask that the Holy Spirit empower you and give you strength in the times you feel discouraged. And I pray that your efforts will provide hope and healing in broken places.

Be brave today. Step out in faith and with God's leading. Know that greatness never comes from staying within your comfort zone. Harness the power of the Holy Spirit and believe that with God, all things are possible. Shine his light into the darkness in our world. When we love as Jesus has loved, we draw others to him and provide the opportunity for him to work miracles in their hearts. So love *everyone* to Jesus and let him do the rest.

VERSES TO ENCOURAGE YOU

Learn to do good; seek justice, correct oppression; bring justice to the fatherless, plead the widow's cause.

—Isaiah 1:17 (ESV)

Instead, I want to see a mighty flood of justice, an endless river of righteous living.

—Amos 5:24

Better a little with righteousness than much gain with injustice.

—Proverbs 16:8 (NIV)

And what does the Lord require of you but to do justice, and to love kindness, and to walk humbly with your God?

—Micah 6:8 (ESV)

SONGS FOR YOUR SOUL

- "By Our Love" by Christy Nockels
- "The Proof of Your Love" by for King & Country
- "Bleed the Same" by Mandisa

A CONVERSATION WITH GOD

Dear God,

My heart breaks as I see people being shamed, rejected, criticized, or even harmed because of being different. Lord, help me be a vessel of change. Give me strength to share in the solution rather than propagate the problem and to be brave enough to bridge the gap, shining your light into these dark situations. Empower me to see each person I encounter as a neighbor worthy of sacrificial love. Give me the courage to sit with them face-to-face and to love them to Jesus. Amen.

NOTES

CHAPTER 18

When You Want to Share Your Faith

And God will generously provide all you need. Then you will always have everything you need and plenty left over to share with others.

—2 CORINTHIANS 9:8

I love Jesus with my whole heart and am beyond grateful for what he has done for me through the cross. Blessed with a gift of faith, I have grown to trust God through life's joys, challenges, and uncertainties. And while I love writing about my faith, the thought of verbally sharing the Gospel face-to-face has always terrified me. How do I start the conversation? How do I find the right words? What will people think? What if I offend them? What if I say the wrong thing and turn someone away from God? Maybe some of these thoughts resonate with you, and perhaps you can add to the list of immobilizing concerns.

These types of questions are all based in fear: fear of perceptions, fear of inadequacy, and fear of failure. Reservations are put into our heads by the enemy, who does not want us to express the importance of God in our lives, share the Gospel, or turn anyone toward a life of trusting the Almighty. In fact, he wants the opposite. And Satan, the grand deceiver, will use any trickery or mind games he can to prevent us from courageously sharing our faith. But we can't let him win.

We are encouraged throughout the Bible that God is with us in all our endeavors, and that includes sharing our faith. As we attempt to block out the taunting voice of the enemy telling us not to reveal the truth of the Gospel, there is a loving and quiet reassurance from God to proceed. He will equip us with the needed words at the time of the conversation: "And God will generously provide all you need. Then you will always have everything you need and plenty left over to share with others" (2 Corinthians 9:8).

Have you felt a holy nudge to share your story of faith? While it may initially be uncomfortable to tell, your story is unlike anyone else's. God has created a beautiful tapestry of people, places, and events that have shaped your life. He carefully winds each thread together with unconditional love, undeserved mercy, and generous grace. The awesome beauty of his divine craftsmanship and power of his love, pinnacled by giving the life of his only Son in exchange for ours, is a tale worth telling. The truth of the way he weaves events to transform you from who you once have been to who you are today, in Christ, can bring much-needed hope to a world of hurting people.

The word *evangelizing*, which means "sharing one's faith," is met with mixed responses. A recent study by the evangelical polling firm the Barna Group has shown that 73 percent of millennials feel equipped to share their faith, and over 95 percent think it's important.[1] But within this generation that embraces diversity and is intentionally sensitive to respecting people's differences, almost half of millennials believe sharing their faith is at least somewhat wrong to do. In our fear of offending someone or of stepping outside our comfort zones, are we leaving the continuation of faith in God in later generations up to chance? Or are we bravely ready to take Jesus at his word when he has told us to "go and make disciples of all the nations"?

How often does God tell us not to give in to fear? It has been said the words *do not be afraid* or *fear not* appear 365 times in the Bible. That provides one scripture for every day of the year, which sounds like a very intentional number from a lovingly intentional God. I don't know about you, but I certainly need those frequent reminders and that encouragement.

Fear-not scriptures are a great place to start preparations for sharing our faith. God reassures us that we are not alone during conversations about our faith. He encourages us to have strength and power through the Holy Spirit to do far more than we may hope or imagine. Rather than giving in to the angst, we need to pause and pray for God to prepare our hearts and minds to share boldly. Pray for the Holy Spirit to give us the right words at the right moment.

Some people are seeking how to live with increased faith, while others don't even believe in a higher power. Our approach to people with these different perspectives will vary. But the constants in the conversations should be gentleness and receptiveness. As the discussions become deeper, our own vulnerability encourages the other person to be vulnerable as well. And it's wise always to pray before the conversation. Pray that we be filled with the Holy Spirit, that we speak courageously, and that our words are pleasing to God.

After spending time in the Word and through prayer, we can then ask God to show us the right person with whom we should gently open up about our faith. We begin by building a deeper and trusting relationship with that person. People are more likely to hear our story when they themselves feel valued and understood. Our genuine heart for them is felt as we ask questions and really take time to hear about their journey without interrupting them.

How do we begin the conversation with someone who is a nonbeliever? We ask insightful, nonthreatening, and caring questions that will require the person to begin to delve into the origin of their beliefs:

- What was growing up like for you?
- What shapes your values and helps provide your moral compass?
- Where do you get strength in difficult times?
- How do you define who you want to be?
- Where do you find hope in life's challenges?

While these questions do not ask specifically about religion, the responses will help us understand how this person's journey has shaped their beliefs. Giving them freedom to share their pain and their victories in a nonjudgmental way sets the stage for a deeper level of authentic sharing. And at some point in the conversation, there is a good chance they will begin to ask us similar questions. This creates the opportunity for us to talk openly and humbly about our faith journey and why it is so important to us.

When talking with someone who already believes but wants a deeper faith, the conversation takes a different path. Asking gentle questions is still a great way to begin the conversation so that we have a greater understanding of their perspective. Many of the same questions will be helpful. We may also ask, "Was faith a part of your family growing up?" or "Have you had any experiences that turned you toward or away from God?" Carefully listening and fully engaging with the person while providing a safe space to express questions provides an intimate environment suited to diving into a discussion of deeper faith.

In being a good listener, we verbally acknowledge that we hear them by reiterating important portions of their story and their feelings. Positive reinforcement, such as "It sounds like you were really hurt" or "That must have been difficult for you," encourages them to continue to be vulnerable. As tempting as it may be to jump in and say, "I had something similar happen," or "I know how you feel because ...," those responses only serve to bring the conversation back to ourselves and can hinder their willingness to share or to be open to our sharing. People want to feel understood and seen before they are willing to be vulnerable.

Being prepared with snippets of our own faith journey and how trusting God has made a monumental difference in our lives gives credence to our testimony. Having an authentic conversation requires being vulnerable ourselves. We can not only share how broken we have been before accepting Christ but also admit to our ongoing imperfection and need for continual grace. Describing how we approach difficult times and giving specific examples of how our God has faithfully helped us through our own life challenges provides much-needed hope.

Friend, it takes patience, gentleness, vulnerability, and courage to have a meaningful discussion about your faith. Instead of listening to the enemy's malevolent distractions and lies, hear your heavenly Father's voice of loving encouragement. Know that he is lifting you and urging you forward. Understand, too, that there are no right or wrong words as long as they are spoken gently, humbly, in truth, and from the heart. As you trust in him, God will skillfully help you navigate the deep waters of sharing your testimony.

So fear not. Release the nagging doubts and seize the Spirit-filled opportunity to share your faith. God has empowered and prepared you for this conversation, friend. You never know how life changing it may be for the other person. But understand that God does know, and that's why he has brought you to this moment. He wants you to courageously share your unique story. And trust that, even if you feel that you have bumbled through it, God will still use your courageous efforts and authentic words for his ultimate glory.

VERSES TO ENCOURAGE YOU

So do not fear, for I am with you; do not be dismayed, for I am your God. I will strengthen you and help you.
—Isaiah 41:10 (NIV)

For God has not given us a spirit of fear and timidity, but of power, love, and self-discipline. So never be ashamed to tell others about our Lord.
—2 Timothy 1:7–8

And if someone asks about your Christian hope, always be ready to explain it. But do this in a gentle and respectful way.
—1 Peter 3:15–16

Each day proclaim the good news that He saves. Publish his glorious deeds among the nations. Tell everyone about the amazing things He does.
—Psalm 96:2–3

SONGS FOR YOUR SOUL

- "Give Me Faith" by Elevation Worship
- "Then Christ Came" by MercyMe
- "Shine" by Newsboys
- "My Story" by Big Daddy Weave

A CONVERSATION WITH GOD

Dear God,

I feel called to share your good news, but I am intimidated. I'm afraid I will be laughed at, be ridiculed, or say the entirely wrong thing. I know that you do not cause this fear inside me, but rather, it comes from the enemy. Give me the courage to follow your lead and the strength to ignore Satan's attempts to thwart my good intentions. Help me further your kingdom by lovingly sharing the truth and light of Jesus Christ in a real and tangible way. In his name, I pray. Amen.

NOTES

CHAPTER 19

When You Need to Heal a Broken Relationship

Make allowance for each other's faults, and forgive anyone who offends you. Remember, the Lord forgave you, so you must forgive others.

—COLOSSIANS 3:13

Life is at its best when we are in harmony with others. Why? Because we have been created to be in relationships. God created Adam so the two could have an intimate relationship. Eve was created to be in relationship with Adam. So from the beginning of time, we have never been meant to go it alone. A journey shared with others, those with whom we feel safe both emotionally and physically, creates the opportunity for us to flourish. Healthy relationships allow both people to feel loved, valued, and encouraged. Within the context of a healthy bond, we can be ourselves yet also be challenged, change, and grow without fear of rejection.

Yet even a healthy relationship, be it with a partner, a parent, or a friend, experiences ups and downs. Because each of us is broken, we aren't always kind or gentle or patient with one another, especially those we love. The close connection we share may provide the opportunity for unchecked conversations. Rash thoughts are spoken aloud. Words are misinterpreted. Feelings are hurt. A once healthy and mutually beneficial relationship begins to feel damaged.

I trust that you are currently hurting because a previously vibrant relationship has become marred. You may be blaming yourself for the separation, or you may be angry at the other party for their role in the situation. Chances are that you are both suffering from some degree of pain and regret. The words *I'm sorry* may put a temporary bandage on the gaping wound, but is this enough to bring about complete healing? Friend, I want you to know that, regardless of your role in the conflict, there is hope for complete reconciliation.

Because we are flawed humans, God has known that we will face challenges in our relationships. He has given us an example in Jesus Christ of how to respond gently and lovingly, despite conflict. Paul reminds us in the New Testament of the importance of forgiving those who have caused us hurt and regaining a harmonious relationship: "Make allowance for each other's faults, and forgive anyone who offends you. Remember, the Lord forgave you, so you must forgive others" (Col. 3:13).

The directive to love others has been spoken by Jesus himself, and how we engage in relationships with other people is the perfect opportunity to live out that command. Agape, the type of love to which Christ calls us, is a selfless devotion that includes sacrificing oneself without complaint, calmness in the face of difficulties, and patience when under pressure. To be truly loving in our relationships can be difficult because this goes against our innate tendency to be self-focused. But love seeks to build bridges rather than widen chasms. Love chooses to honor and respect other people, even when they have viewpoints different from our own. Those differences are often the cause of wedges in our relationships.

In the middle of a heated exchange or passive-aggressive silence, the thought of forgiveness is not typically at the forefront of our vengeful minds. If you are encumbered by a broken relationship, you can likely attest that the thoughts racing through your brain are not filled with butterflies and rainbows. Our self-protective tendencies and defense mechanisms can create solid barriers to the chance of reconciliation. So how can we actively seek to regain the harmony that has once existed?

The first step is to realistically evaluate the relationship to determine that it is one worth saving. Please understand that the following is not a discussion for toxic relationships, which are "characterized by behaviors on the part of the toxic partner that are emotionally and, not infrequently, physically damaging to their partner. A toxic relationship is characterized by insecurity, self-centeredness, dominance and control."[1] If you are in an ongoing and consistently toxic relationship, I encourage you to seek professional help and guidance to ensure your safety and to return to a place of self-worth and self-love.

Even in healthy relationships, we all make mistakes. The goal is to learn from our errors and not follow the same path of harmful behaviors in the future. Understanding that your friend, spouse, or relative is also a flawed human can bring about the beginnings of a compassionate response. In the New Testament book of Matthew, Jesus gives precise direction and guidance for initiating the healing of broken relationships: "If another believer sins against you, go privately and point out the offense. If the other person listens and confesses it, you have won that person back" (18:15).

Many have experienced an acceleration of anger and frustration when ruminating over a perceived wrong. The more we think about it, the angrier and more hurt we become. Reliving the offense over and over in our minds can lead to an escalation or exaggeration of the event. It serves to create an even bigger wedge in an already fractured bond. Reconciling a broken relationship is impossible on our own. The two parties involved must both willingly engage in healing. It requires a conversation, best done face-to-face, to begin the restoration process.

To regain the balance in a previously healthy relationship, Melanie Greenberg, PhD, has developed the HEAL technique, which replaces defensive self-protection with compassionate presence and loving connection.[2]

1. **Hear.** When the other party speaks, remain mentally present and intentionally listen to all they are saying and showing us through body language. Are they angry, hurt, or sad? Where are they feeling unvalued, criticized, or misunderstood? While

our initial instinct may be to formulate a rebuttal or tune out an uncomfortable interaction, this will lead only to further distancing and alienation. When we don't feel heard, we don't feel valued.

2. **Empathize.** Allow the experience of our partner, spouse, family member, or friend to affect us deeply. Trying to put ourselves in their shoes will help us understand the hidden feelings they may be experiencing. We sometimes express anger when the underlying feeling is hurt, worry, or sadness. According to Greenberg, "Your first instinct in hearing your partner's distress may be to try to solve the problem or give advice. Often, however, this advice comes across as critical or judgmental, which can make things worse." Instead, we need to have compassion for their feelings, stay emotionally engaged, and truly try to understand their perspective.

3. **Act.** We must next take action toward reconciliation. This involves acknowledging our role in the distancing, making a commitment to address the other's concerns, and showing a willingness to change. Following through on the issues identified in our conversation helps the other person feel respected and appreciated.

4. **Love.** We show love by making time in our busy schedule to reconnect lovingly, recalling the positive qualities that have initially brought the two of us together. We must forgive ourselves and the other party for mistakes that have been made and feelings that have been hurt. Providing unconditional love through our words and actions creates the needed conduit for reconciliation.

Strained relationships are rarely the fault of one party, though one person may have inflicted the initial wound that has begun the downward spiral. I gently encourage you to honestly explore your role in the woundedness. Admitting when you may have been wrong, being vulnerable and authentic, and taking accountability for your actions create trust and work toward restoring a broken relationship. Opening the door to a healthy conversation paves the way to forgiveness and ultimately reconciliation. It takes work. But in the end, the "HEAL-ing" of a beloved friendship or meaningful relationship is well worth the time and effort.

God fully understands the complexities and challenges we experience in relationships. He has great compassion for his people, and that includes you. As you honestly and gently explore your role in a disagreement, pray for his compassion. Even if you feel the other person is at fault, be willing to make the first difficult move toward conflict resolution. We most beautifully live out Jesus's calling to love when our primary goal in relationships is to seek peace and harmony.

Take your broken relationship before God, my friend. Ask him for understanding, guidance, and patience through the restoration process. Trust in him that all things are possible when bathed in his love and forgiveness. Be willing to be a selfless vessel of kindness, gentleness, forgiveness, and hope. Then take the first bold step toward healing.

VERSES TO ENCOURAGE YOU

Always be humble and gentle. Be patient with each other, making allowance for each other's faults because of your love. Make every effort to keep yourselves united in the Spirit, binding yourselves together with peace.
—Ephesians 4:2–3

For God was in Christ, reconciling the world to himself, no longer counting people's sins against them. And he gave us this wonderful message of reconciliation.
—2 Corinthians 5:19

You must all be quick to listen, slow to speak, and slow to get angry. Human anger does not produce the righteousness God desires.
—James 1:19

Be gentle with one another, sensitive. Forgive one another as quickly and thoroughly as God in Christ forgave you.

—Ephesians 4:32 (MSG)

SONGS FOR YOUR SOUL

- "Come As You Are" by Crowder
- "Restore" by Chris August
- "I Will Be Your Friend" by Michael W. Smith

A CONVERSATION WITH GOD

Dear God,

Give me courage, humility, and compassion to heal this relationship. Help me seek to listen rather than to be heard. Give me patience to truly understand the other perspective so that we can heal, learn, and grow together. Fill me to overflowing with your love so that it spills into all my relationships. Help me be a vessel of restoration and reconciliation. In Jesus's name, amen.

NOTES

CHAPTER 20

When You Feel Moved to Make a Difference

Learn to do good. Seek justice. Help the oppressed. Defend
the cause of the orphans. Fight for the rights of widows.
—ISAIAH 1:17

We live in a broken world full of broken people in broken places. Only in heaven will we see complete healing, unadulterated love, and God's full peace. But the Lord relies on his children here on the earth to bring a glimpse of that healing, love, and peace to others to change lives and bring people to Jesus. Sr. Mary Rose McGeady, known for her extensive work with homeless youth at Covenant House in New York City, has captured the heart of selfless service when she has said, "There is no greater reward than to make a fundamental difference in someone's life."

Have you been touched to the core by a personal or painful story you have heard? Where have you seen people or situations that are heartbreaking to you? When have you felt nudged to support a charitable cause? Have you recently encountered someone suffering through a personal illness or tragedy? What has God lain on your heart that wrecks your soul and you can't seem to shake?

It takes insight to understand that these situations tugging on your heart are not an accident. They are often a divine gift, friend, giving rise to a dormant desire to make a positive difference and improve the greater good. While you may not be certain that you can make a significant impact, most rewards in life require stepping courageously out of the comfort of the present into an unsure but hopeful future.

We are reminded throughout the Bible of God's desire for us to love, encourage, and help one another: "Learn to do good. Seek justice. Help the oppressed. Defend the cause of the orphans. Fight for the rights of widows" (Isa. 1:17). Focusing on how we may help with others' problems can realign our perspective and diminish the importance of our own issues.

Although the purpose in service is to selflessly help others, there are many proven personal benefits to those who serve. Participating in volunteer activities improves both mental and physical health, decreasing stress, anxiety, and depression while reducing mortality rates.[1] In addition to providing a feeling of purpose, volunteering teaches new skills and nurtures relationships, developing a sense of belonging. Increased life satisfaction and happiness are also seen in those who work to make a positive difference in the lives of others.[2]

While many causes have touched my spirit, I find those involving children to be the most heart wrenching. Too many children suffer unthinkable cruelty, often at the hands of trusted adults. Whether this is physical, emotional, or sexual abuse, the results are devastating. Exploitation of children for personal gain or satisfaction, leading to their lifelong trauma, has the Lord grabbing at my heart and not letting go.

Human trafficking is the largest growing global criminal industry, with estimates of revenue reaching a staggering $150 billion. One conservative estimate indicates there are currently twenty-seven million enslaved sufferers worldwide, and one in every three is a child. While it's estimated that 1.2 million children are trafficked each year, the reality is likely much grimmer.[3, 4] The use of social media in exploitation has dramatically increased to recruit and advertise the services of victims. Coercion, intimidation, physical and emotional abuse, fear, and shame are all tactics traffickers use to prevent the victims from leaving bondage. (If this cause touches your heart as well, you can find ways to help at http://knottoday.org.)

The Bible provides clear condemnation for this and other types of oppression: "Help him to defend the poor, to rescue the children of the needy, and to crush their oppressors" (Ps. 72:4). In the Gospel of Luke, Jesus proclaims that he is the Savior the people have been awaiting when he reads from the scroll: "The Spirit of the Lord is upon me, for he has anointed me to bring Good News to the poor. He has sent me to proclaim that captives be released, that the blind will see, that the oppressed will be set free" (4:18). In both the Old Testament and the New Testament, God leaves no doubt that he is strongly opposed to people and systems that cause persecution or oppression to any of his beloved people.

Not only does Jesus speak of physical blindness but we also are all too frequently blind to the many people who are oppressed or in need in our local communities, in our nation, and around the world. Once that veil is lifted, once we begin to truly see the undeserved plight of others, it is hard to stay put and do nothing. Once God opens our heart to someone else's vulnerability and harsh reality, he often also encourages us to do something about it.

Perhaps you feel moved to make a difference but don't have a clear idea of how you want to serve. Do not feel discouraged in the uncertainty. Intentionally keeping your eyes and ears open to people around you will almost always give needed direction. Also, pray for guidance in your search and consider exploring local opportunities to serve at websites such as http://volunteermatch.org. Having a compassionate and open heart provides fertile ground for the Lord to plant the seed of empathy in an area in which you can cultivate help, hope, and healing.

When God urges us into a ministry of helping others, it is an honor. It may mean jumping in even if we don't feel ready for the task. But when we put off nudges from the Lord, we risk never venturing into his calling. We risk missing an opportunity to affect the lives of others in a way that only we can. We miss the chance to be a life-changing blessing to someone else.

You may have the opportunity to invite other people into charitable service as well. They can be greatly encouraged by your enthusiasm over the positive impact you have witnessed through serving others. The goal isn't to be prideful in telling what benevolent acts you have accomplished. The objective is to plant seeds of hope, cultivate selfless and generous hearts, and bear fruit by doing good deeds in the name of Jesus.

Remember that God doesn't call the equipped; he equips the called. So, friend, bathe your prompting in prayer and allow him to lead you on the path toward bringing the situation to light and to effecting positive change. Don't wait until you are less busy, you are done with a work project, the kids are grown, or you feel prepared. Life is full of too real, and too many, excuses. Instead, put this issue that has been laid on your heart near the top of your priority list. Begin the process of connecting this week. I don't believe you will ever regret it.

God will absolutely bless you as you bless others. While that shouldn't be the reason to move, it is a wonderful and unexpected reward. So don't hesitate. Don't procrastinate. Reach up for divine direction and reach out in faith. Prepare to be amazed at what God can do in you and through you when you follow his holy nudges to be a selfless vessel of hope for someone else. You, my friend, are a blessing waiting to happen.

VERSES TO ENCOURAGE YOU

May he give you the power to accomplish all the good things your faith prompts you to do.
—2 Thessalonians 1:11

Be fair-minded and just. Do what is right! Help those who have been robbed; rescue them from their oppressors.
—Jeremiah 22:3

So, let's not get tired of doing what is good. At just the right time, we will reap a harvest of blessing if we don't give up.
—Galatians 6:9

Our people must learn to do good by meeting the urgent needs of others.
—Titus 3:14

SONGS FOR YOUR SOUL

- "Do Something" by Matthew West
- "Hosanna" by Hillsong United
- "God of Justice" by Tim Hughes

A CONVERSATION WITH GOD

Dear God,

There is so much pain and suffering in our world. While I don't always feel prepared, I want to help! God, please break my heart for what breaks yours. Give me the conviction, the courage, and the perseverance to make a difference. Help me love others, seek to stop oppression, and work to rescue those who are in dark or lonely places in their lives. Help me be your light. In Jesus's name, amen.

NOTES

CHAPTER 21

When You Need to Make an Important Decision

For God is working in you, giving you the desire and the power to do what pleases him.
— PHILIPPIANS 2:13

L ife is full of choices. Some of them are easy, and some tear at our gut as we try to make the right decision. Small daily choices may come easily, but the decisions that have the potential to change the trajectory of our lives are much more challenging. It is in making these profound choices that we can find ourselves feeling full of stress, worry, and anxiety.

What college should I attend? Which career path should I choose? Which job offer is the best for me? Is this the person I should marry? Should we have or adopt a child? What city should we live in? When should I retire? These types of potentially life-changing decisions require deep thought and prayer.

As you face the decision before you, I encourage taking ample time to ponder before pouncing. Too often we are tempted or pressured to jump into a vital decision quickly rather than giving it the full thought process it deserves. Your success in having made good choices in the past can reassure you that you can thoroughly think through the options and choose wisely. And if you've felt plagued by poor decisions in the past, you now have the opportunity to approach a situation differently.

Our heavenly Father understands that life on the earth is challenging. He has given us free will to make choices throughout our lives and provides scripture for encouragement. Yet he also knows that we won't always make the best choices. In Acts 14:22, we are reminded that we must suffer hardships but are encouraged to continue in the faith. A verse that I have found helpful during times of challenge or difficult choices has been Proverbs 3:5–6: "Trust in the Lord with all your heart; do not depend on your own understanding. Seek his will in all you do, and he will show you which path to take." While prayer and trusting God are critical, using a practical approach to decision-making can help the process seem less overwhelming.

The University of Massachusetts Dartmouth is one of many institutions that has outlined the steps of an effective decision-making process.[1] Following an intentional process helps organize the relevant information while weeding out distractors so we can choose the best alternative at that time. After acting on the selection, the final step is to stand back and evaluate the decision and the consequences. This reflection allows us to learn from the choice, even if it turns out to be a poor decision. As author Mark Twain has said, "Good decisions come from experience. Experience comes from making bad decisions."

The first step in making a good decision is to identify the goal and write it down. While this may sound obvious and simple, it is easy to lose sight of the big picture after looking at all the options. When considering each choice, refer back to the primary goal. Any possibility that does not directly align with the defined objective should be excluded. Following this essential step can prevent emotions from leading us to a poor decision.

Next, outline your standards and morals. Try to create the list with purposeful thought and without emotional influence. Ask yourself, *What are the minimum acceptable criteria?* Then gather information about each alternative. Do any of the options go against your values? What principles are you not willing to compromise? Defining these objectives and writing them down can also help narrow the list of possibilities.

Third, reflect on previous experiences. Throughout our lives, we learn from the results of decisions we have made, both the good and the bad. What has led to a poor choice? Have we lost sight of the goal or forgotten to adhere to our minimum standards? Have we allowed emotion to rule the decision? Have we rushed into a choice that requires more time and thought? Sometimes the best knowledge gained is from making a poor choice, understanding what has led to it, and learning from the mistake.

Does our chosen path align with God's desires for his people? Is the decision directly answered in scripture? If not, is there a trusted pastor or other person who can help us understand whether the scriptures can guide our evaluation process? In Isaiah 46:10 (NIV), the Lord reminds us that he knows the ending well before we do and that his "purposes stand." We can take comfort in knowing that even if we don't always make the best choice, God can use it for good.

Have there been any warning signs? At times, we can get so caught up in the pressure or excitement of making a decision that we ignore red flags or wise counsel against certain actions. Taking our time to process all options wisely rather than acting hastily can prevent difficulties in the future. When we are walking in God's will, we should not feel heavily burdened or uneasy about moving forward. Rather, when he is guiding our steps, there is often a feeling of lightness, certainty, and peace as the Holy Spirit prods us in the right direction.

Most importantly, we must commit the vital decisions in our lives to intense prayer. Attempts to proceed independently from God can lead to heartache and poor outcomes. Is there any angst or opposition as we move toward one option? This is often a divine admonition to step back and reconsider. Pray for God to close the doors to any choice that is not in alignment with his desires and to throw the gate wide open to the best option: "For God is working in you, giving you the desire and the power to do what pleases him" (Phil. 2:13). Know that because God truly wants what is best for us, in pleasing him with our choices, we also allow him to fully move within our lives.

We can also consider asking a trusted friend to pray about the decision with us and for us. Asking others to pray as we contemplate can bring clarity as they reveal any divine answers they hear. We may then prayerfully narrow our options down to the final choice and quietly listen for the Lord's response and confirmation. It's important to understand that moving in the path of God's will during our lives often brings a sense of calm to the heart and soul. That internal tranquility is the signal we have chosen wisely and can bring peace in moving forward.

The unknown future often brings fear with it. Don't allow the thought of a difficult decision to numb you to the point of inaction. Begin your processing today by writing down your intended personal goal and moral standards. As you move through each step of the decision process, remember to return to those written words again and again. Once you have prayerfully made your choice, confidently proceed in that direction. Defy the temptation to spend too much time rethinking, overprocessing, and second-guessing, which can lead to decision paralysis and never moving forward. Instead, trust yourself and the inner tranquility from God as you push ahead.

Surrendering your life and decisions fully to the Lord takes practice, my friend. Yet it is a fruitful endeavor that results in a closer relationship with the Lord, embodied by greater trust and increased faith. Even if the outcome of the decision is not perfect, there are always lessons to be learned. And the benefit of a closer relationship with your heavenly Father, as you trust in him, *is* a perfect win.

It's OK to feel scared yet excited to commit to a life decision with such profound impact. While the Lord gives you freedom to choose, he always wants you to opt for the most fulfilling path—the one that brings you closer to your true purpose and to him. Learning to trust him in the small decisions makes it easier to rely on God in the colossal ones. So believe his assurances. Make the decision. Then step faithfully and confidently into the future that awaits.

VERSES TO ENCOURAGE YOU

The Lord says, "I will guide you along the best pathway for your life. I will advise you and watch over you."

—Psalm 32:8

If you need wisdom, ask our generous God, and he will give it to you. He will not rebuke you for asking.

—James 1:5

Trust in the Lord with all your heart; do not depend on your own understanding. Seek his will in all you do, and he will show you which path to take.

—Proverbs 3:5–6

Don't be afraid, for I am with you. Don't be discouraged, for I am your God. I will strengthen you and help you.

—Isaiah 41:10

SONGS FOR YOUR SOUL

- "Oceans (Where Feet May Fail)" by Hillsong United
- "Where You Lead Me" by MercyMe

A CONVERSATION WITH GOD

Dear God,

I am standing at a crossroads and uncertain of the direction to move. I see pros and cons for each path, and this paralyzes me. What if I make the wrong choice? Father, I need your clear guidance and wisdom. Help me make the best decision not only for me but also to further your kingdom. Give me the courage to take one step at a time into the future you have for me, confident that your plans for me are good. Thank you for your unfailing love. Amen.

NOTES

CHAPTER 22

When You Want to Sing God's Praises

Sing to the Lord; praise his name. Each day proclaim the good news that he saves.

—PSALM 96:2

While we all face challenges in life, we also experience many blessings. In times of darkness or despair, it can be nearly impossible to focus on positive aspects of life. Hallelujah for the times that we can clearly see God at work in our lives! Whether a new job offer, an engagement, a graduation, the birth of a child, clear guidance for needed direction, a beautiful sunset, a work accomplished, a piece of good news, or a multitude of other joys, there are many moments when we just want to say, "Praise God!"

Are you experiencing a mountaintop moment or other type of great joy? What a glorious gift! Don't be reluctant or afraid to praise the Lord for his faithfulness. Whether in private or with others, it's good to acknowledge and thank God for his abundant generosity and our many blessings: "Sing to the Lord; praise his name. Each day proclaim the good news that he saves" (Ps. 96:2).

Reflecting on life's blessings naturally leads to a state of gratitude, especially when we acknowledge that they are truly undeserved. Robert Emmons, the world's leading expert on gratitude research, reports physical, emotional, and social benefits from thankfulness. Gratitude is associated with a stronger immune system, better sleep, fewer aches and pains, and lower blood pressure. As dopamine is released, people also experience more joy, pleasure, alertness, and optimism. Social benefits include feeling more compassion for others, being more forgiving, and feeling less isolated. Finally, grateful people are also more resistant to stress and have a greater sense of self-worth.[1]

What joys are you experiencing that bring you to a place of gratitude and praise? Have you had an affirming answer to prayer? Has God displayed his goodness as you experience a victory? Are you clearly seeing the wonder of his creations in the world or people around you? Whether a small daily blessing or an enormous miracle, journaling or vocalizing thanks to the Lord not only brings him joy but also produces the described neurophysiological benefits.

Throughout scripture, we see thankfulness displayed. King David provides an authentic example of a relationship with the Lord, unashamedly crying out to God with both his woes and his joys. After a victorious effort over his enemies, David exclaims, "I will praise you, Lord, with all my heart; I will tell of all the marvelous things you have done. I will be filled with joy because of you" (Ps. 9:1–2).

My husband, Jon, was recently in his room at a hotel when he heard loud yelling near the outdoor pool. After looking out the window and realizing that people were attempting to do CPR on someone, he raced down to help. Poolside, he found a group of people standing helplessly around a blue man who had clearly been pulled from the water. As a physician, my husband quickly assessed the young man, only to find no pulse or breathing, and began performing CPR while an ambulance was called.

A community of the victim's friends and family surrounded him with love and support, speaking encouraging words while rubbing his hands and feet. After several minutes of Jon and our son-in-law, Joe, performing CPR, their hope for his recovery was waning. They persisted, however, while a friend of the young man gave him breaths. Shockingly, after a full seven minutes of resuscitative efforts, a pulse was found. The twenty-six-year-old man, still unconscious, was breathing on his own.

The next day, security camera footage showed that the man had been underwater for five minutes before being rescued, and it was nearly two additional minutes before Jon had arrived at the scene. All in all, the young man, named Paras, was without pulse or respirations for about fourteen minutes, suggesting a very grim prognosis. He was placed on life support at the hospital and then airlifted to a high-level trauma center for further care.

Prayer chains were started. By the third day, Paras was in a medically induced coma to allow his body to heal, and our hopes for his recovery were slim. Doctors confirmed that he had almost no chance for meaningful survival without brain damage. Prayer circles were widened. The medical team prepared friends and family for the worst, stating that Paras was not expected to survive. Then the awesome power of prayer became evident.

On the fourth day, the doctors lightened the sedative medication and found that Paras could blink and squeeze hands on command. They were stunned to find that his brain scan was nearly normal, and his organs were functioning well. Prayer chains were updated with the hopeful news. Because he was not yet out of the woods, intense prayers continued from areas around the globe. On the sixth day, Paras was off the ventilator and talking. On the ninth day, he was walking and was moved from the intensive care unit. A few days later, Paras was released to return home. This young man went on to defeat all odds and make a full recovery.

Medical professionals were in disbelief. Family and friends who had been preparing for the worst were overjoyed. The prayer community was elated to witness such a huge answer to big and bold prayers. Today Paras expresses immense thankfulness to God, the people who rescued and revived him, and all those who prayed on his behalf. It was a miraculous recovery, God's miracle. This was definitely a time to shout, "Hallelujah!"

And yet do we really need an evident miracle to sing God's praises? Caught up in the busyness of day-to-day life, we sometimes fail to truly appreciate the miracle of God's goodness and faithfulness. And the best news for each of us is one often taken for granted. We tend to forget the saving grace that God consistently provides as we seek him.

Each Christmas season we are reminded of the enormous sacrifice God has made by coming to the earth, wrapped in human flesh as a vulnerable infant, to rescue each of us from our lives of sin. His plan wasn't to send an angel to save the world; he humbly came himself. God didn't say, "I'll come to you when you deserve it," or "Work hard, and then I will offer you grace." No, God came when humanity was thick with sin, broken, and in desperate need of a Savior. He came at exactly the right time, over two thousand years ago, to begin the movement of miraculous love and grace through the body of Jesus Christ.

Today is a day for celebration. "This is the day the Lord has made. We will rejoice and be glad in it" (Ps. 118:24). Begin by appreciating beauty in the small details of life. Rejoice for the undeserved blessings you have received. Shout of God's goodness and faithfulness from the mountaintops. And yes, sing his praises aloud for others to hear, sharing the amazing news of our heavenly Father's power, grace, and generosity poured out for all his children.

Oh, it's not that we don't recognize and appreciate an obvious miracle when we see or hear about one. Those moments or stories will be indelibly ingrained in our minds and hearts. They are proof that God exists and is actively and lovingly at work in our lives. They also stand in evidence to the wondrous power of prayer.

But your everyday miracles are just as significant. So whatever you are celebrating today, don't hold back. Openly express gratitude to your heavenly Father, who gives so generously. Sing his praises, for hallelujah, you worship a good and faithful and miraculous God!

VERSES TO ENCOURAGE YOU

Sing for joy, O heavens! Rejoice, O earth! Burst into song, O mountains! For the Lord has comforted his people and will have compassion on them in their suffering.
—Isaiah 49:13

Let all that I am praise the Lord; with my whole heart, I will praise his holy name. Let all that I am praise the Lord; may I never forget the good things he does for me.

—Psalm 103:1–2

I will meditate on your majestic, glorious splendor and your wonderful miracles.

—Psalm 145:5

Worship the Lord with gladness. Come before him, singing with joy.

—Psalm 100:2

SONGS FOR YOUR SOUL

- "How Great Is Our God" by Chris Tomlin
- "Your Great Name" by Natalie Grant
- "Promises" by Maverick City Music

A CONVERSATION WITH GOD

Dear God,

You are so good! I am amazed at your creation as I take in the beauty of a sunrise, hear the laughter of a child, or feel the power in the wind, reminding me of your Holy Spirit. I am in awe of your kindness, compassion, and mercies, which are new each morning. Thank you for being the one constant in my life. Thank you because when people disappoint, I can still trust in you. May I sing your praises, God, and may I glorify you all my days so that others may come to know and trust you as well. In Jesus's name, amen.

NOTES

CHAPTER 23

When You Are Struggling with Pride or Feel like Boasting

Don't be selfish; don't try to impress others. Be humble, thinking of others as better than yourselves.
— PHILIPPIANS 2:3

*B*oasting, bragging, self-enhancement— these terms, often interchangeable, refer to excessively proud or boastful talk about one's achievements or possessions. Some people fall into this pattern of conversation without realizing it, but harmful consequences can occur. Attorney and American diplomat Owen D. Young has once said, "When boasting ends, there dignity begins."

What leads to bragging, and what is the result of the behavior? People who brag may be highly sensitive to criticism and can have surprisingly fragile or low self-esteem. While appearing confident and self-assured, they are often seeking approval not received from a parent, partner, or friend. Words of affirmation may be their primary love language,[1] and they may require frequent praise to feel worthwhile.

Do any of these descriptions ring true for you? Are some of your life circumstances leading you to a temptation to brag? It takes an enormous amount of self-awareness, and sometimes the gentle observations from a trusted friend or family member, to realize when we have fallen into this type of self-inflationary behavior. Is it possible that you have plunged into a boastful pattern without even recognizing it? And better yet, are you at a place in your heart and mind to instead choose modesty?

Throughout the Bible, we are reminded to be humble and focus more on others than ourselves. We are repeatedly called to selflessly put others' needs above our own, but this is not an easy task for most of us. By keeping our attention outwardly focused, we diminish the inclination to boast about ourselves: "Don't be selfish; don't try to impress others. Be humble, thinking of others as better than yourselves" (Phil. 2:3). Focusing on the successes and needs of other people helps us step back for a healthier perspective of what is truly important in life.

Excessive boasting can have detrimental effects on marriages, friendships, and interactions with coworkers. Being the person who always must control a conversation or one-up someone else exudes inauthenticity and can create wedges in relationships. According to a *Wall Street Journal* review of articles on the topic,[2] research has shown that braggarts can be viewed as narcissistic and less moral. Additionally, boastful women are typically judged more harshly than boastful men. The result of "harmless" sharing of one's successes may be perceived as arrogance, emotionally distancing us from others or driving away those from whom we seek approval.

Professor and communications expert Preston Ni, MSBA, describes the eight characteristics of narcissistic communicators. These people hoard conversation time, try to control exchanges through frequent interruptions, and often have a false superiority complex. They are seen as unempathetic listeners who engage in "humble bragging, or dramatizing their supposedly envy-worthy lifestyle, praiseworthy achievements, attention-worthy dramas, and status-/trophy-worthy relationships."[3] Narcissistic communicators often come across as know-it-alls, regularly providing unsolicited advice. These behaviors are seen as disingenuous, frequently alienating those they are trying to impress.

Biblical wisdom throughout both the Old Testament and New Testament encourages us to be humble rather than boastful. The Lord desires for us to have close and meaningful relationships with other people, and boasting can get in the way. Scripture warns of the perils of many evils, including being prideful or bragging: "How long will they speak with arrogance? How long will these evil people boast? They crush your people, Lord, hurting those you claim as your own" (Ps. 94:4–5).

Jesus models for us complete humility and asks that we allow him to teach us to be "humble and gentle at heart" (Matt. 11:29). Humility requires avoiding the urge to take credit for something, even if we have a hand in the positive outcome. Being humble allows the soul's pure beauty to radiate and God's light to shine through. Being gentle at heart, mild mannered, and kind creates the opportunity for others to feel seen and heard in our presence. Humility and gentleness don't require a grand entrance and don't seek to be center stage. Rather, these qualities allow us to take several steps away from the spotlight and put others first. They allow us to be giving, selfless, and fruitful for God's kingdom.

It is unlikely that our goal in sharing a personal success, recent purchase, impressive acquaintance, or child's accomplishment is to crush a relationship. Yet we must introspectively evaluate whether this has become a habit and pattern rather than a rare occurrence in our conversations. The following are some questions to consider when we feel the urge to boast:

- What is the motive in sharing this piece of information?
- Will it enhance our relationship in any way?
- Is it worth potentially damaging the relationship to boast about this?
- Is it possible to be humble and share this piece of information?
- What does God want us to do in this situation?

It helps to have a plan of action when we are tempted to brag. The first step may be to engage in honest self-reflection to recognize when our words may have been perceived as boasting. Beware if thoughts take us to phrases such as "Well, I only wanted to …" or "I thought she would be happy for me if …" or "They should know it was my idea to …." When we need to justify our words, there is a good chance they will be ill received.

Next, it's helpful to prepare a *freeze phrase*, something to say to ourselves when we are on the verge of what can be perceived as boasting to make us stop and reconsider. It may be *just listen* or *show love*, whatever will make us stop, pause, and think before speaking. Author Bob Goff suggests saying under our breath, "It's not about me." He encourages us to "say it a dozen times a day. Say it a thousand times a month ... Make it your anthem."[4] We can use this encouraging self-talk to pause purposely and think through our words any time we are ready to jump into a conversation.

Finally, we need to be intentional in our communications. Slowing our day and thoughts allows us to be fully present. As we practice truly listening to other people instead of preparing in our heads what we want to say next, we invite them into a genuine connection. Maintaining eye contact and repeating aloud key phrases they have spoken to gain clarity are acknowledgments that we truly hear them. Asking questions rather than redirecting the conversation to ourselves encourages more sharing. These types of interactions build relationships that are meaningful and mutually beneficial.

Practicing humility is a beautiful antidote to bragging. It often isn't easy, especially when we are excited to share something. But it is God's way. Being humble and gentle requires deliberately putting others before ourselves, buttoning our lips, and allowing others to shine. Humility is encouraging to others and helps us fix our "thoughts on what is true, and honorable, and pure, and lovely, and admirable" (Phil. 4:8).

Today be intentional in engaging in healthy conversations without ever turning the topic to you. If you acknowledge a struggle with narcissistic communication tendencies, this may take great effort. Yet with honest self-reflection and determination, it can become almost second nature as you develop healthy conversational techniques. Humility may not come easily. But with God's help, it is a trait that can be practiced and learned. And in the long run, you will be seen as a better coworker, friend, or partner.

The apostle Paul encourages the people of Corinth to lead lives worthy of Jesus's calling by loving others well, and we are called to do the same: "Love is patient and kind. Love is not jealous or boastful or proud or rude" (1 Cor. 13:4). Take the opportunity in conversations to show love by being a generous listener. It may feel uncomfortable at times, but loving well shows respect for others and builds a bridge in the gap of a society too often focused on selfish promotion.

Pray for God to reveal any prideful tendencies you may have and for protection against the temptation to boast. Pray for healthier communication in all your interactions. Seek more to listen to others than to be heard and find ways to congratulate other people on their achievements. Being authentically present for others creates the opportunity for more genuine and meaningful relationships. What a wonderful reward!

Instead of boasting today, friend, sing praises to your heavenly Father for what you have accomplished and allow his pride to sustain you. Thank him privately for the plentiful provision that has allowed you to make a purchase. Secretly acknowledge his generosity and faithfulness in your triumphs. Praise him for your spouse and children and their successes. Showing gratitude to him alone for all your blessings helps take the credit from you and place it with the Lord, the Giver of all things, where it truly belongs. Then lavishly share his love by bringing a humbler, gentler, and more selflessly compassionate version of yourself to those around you. While they soak in that life-giving love, the ultimate reward from the Father in heaven is yours.

VERSES TO ENCOURAGE YOU

Let someone else praise you, not your own lips.
—Proverbs 27:2

God's Message: "Don't let the wise brag of their wisdom. Don't let the heroes brag of their exploits. Don't let the rich brag of their riches. If you brag, brag of this and this only: that you understand and know me."
—Jeremiah 9:23–24 (MSG)

Finally, all of you, be like-minded, be sympathetic, love one another, be compassionate and humble.
—1 Peter 3:8 (NIV)

SONGS FOR YOUR SOUL

- "Lay Down My Pride" by Jeremy Camp
- "Empty Me" by Chris Sligh

A CONVERSATION WITH GOD

Dear God,

I admit that I struggle with pride. It seems that the norm in our culture is to brag or try to impress people. Remind me to pause before speaking and to search my motives. Help me be an authentic listener and generous communicator. I am so grateful for the many blessings you have given me in my life. Allow that gratitude to be enough. If I must boast, let it be only of you and your goodness, Lord. Amen.

NOTES

CHAPTER 24

When Nothing Seems to Be Going Right

Come to me, all of you who are weary and carry heavy burdens, and I will give you rest.

—MATTHEW 11:28

A re you feeling pushed to the limit? Do you find yourself at the end of your emotional rope because you can't seem to get one single break? Nothing is going the way you have hoped, planned, or envisioned. You may feel overwhelmed, drowning in a sea of stress, defeated, ready to give up. Living through the coronavirus pandemic, which began in 2020, has felt very much like that for many of us, and it has been both exhausting and discouraging.

While an inner voice may be telling you that you are weak or worthless for not being able to conquer the circumstances at hand, please know that intimidating voice is not speaking truth and is not from God. We all walk through times of extreme challenge that are disheartening and demoralizing. Even though we may feel like giving up on ourselves or giving in to the looming depression, there is a light at the end of this long and tortuous tunnel of events. Don't give up, my friend. Trust that the tides will turn at some point, returning you to a place of more hope and greater inner peace.

While in the throes of a stressful or painful season, leaning on our faith can be especially challenging. As our world seems to be spinning in a cycle of negativity, we may have the tendency to try harder and harder to make things go our way. "I *know* I can turn this around if I just ...," we may say. Or alternatively, we may decide to stop trying altogether: "I give up!" Yet these mindsets create the likelihood of more fatigue and further discouragement. Surrendering our circumstances to the Lord, while not an easy task, prepares our heart for whatever comes next. Jesus has said, "Come to me, all of you who are weary and carry heavy burdens, and I will give you rest" (Matt. 11:28).

Discouragement is a psychological response resulting from a disparity between expectations and an event that seems to decrease the chance of that expectation becoming a reality. One resultant problem is that, when disappointed, we may veer from the road of thoughtful processing and constructive steps that can eventually lead to the desired outcome. So while factors beyond our control may have thwarted potential opportunities, it's our response to those factors, positive or negative, that ultimately determines the result.

Negativity bias is described as a cognitive bias that results in adverse events having a more significant impact on our psychological state than positive ones.[1] These negative associations can occur even when the positive event is of the same magnitude. A negativity bias results from spending a great deal of time pontificating over minor frustrations, causing us to ignore positive aspects of our days. Psychologist Barbara Fredrickson has shown that positivity, on the other hand, has many beneficial effects, such as less stress, better cardiovascular health,[2] an improved immune system, and better sleep patterns.

Discouragement is classically attributed to decreases in dopamine and serotonin levels in the brain. Newer research has also shown disappointment to affect the neurochemical balance in the brain through increases in the amounts of the neurotransmitters GABA and glutamate. "The more glutamate is released relative to GABA, the greater the 'disappointment' signal in the brain is likely to be."[3] Serotonin, which is increased with mood elevators, helps balance the negative effects of GABA and glutamate. According to Steven Shabel, PhD, "We may now have a precise neurochemical explanation for why antidepressants make some people more resilient to negative experiences."

Yet not everyone experiencing disappointment requires antidepressants to lift their mood. We can look at these unexpected life setbacks as roadblocks or as detours. Discouragement occurs when we see these incidences as roadblocks. Roadblocks with Do Not Enter signs tell us to stop and go back, and setbacks in life can make us want to stop as well. We may feel there is no use in going forward, giving in to the negative narrative that nothing ever goes as we have planned. We doubt that we can accomplish our goal and feel there is no use even attempting to proceed forward. When we lose the desire to try, this can then become a self-fulfilling prophecy of failure.

A detour, however, tells us to find another way. The expected or desired result isn't completely lost but needs to be found via an alternative path. When we are driving and come to a road detour, frustration is often the immediate response: "I'm on a tight schedule!" or "This isn't in my plan!" or "I'm going to be late!" Yet at times, the detour takes us in a more scenic direction or shows an alternate route we haven't known existed and can be useful later. It requires us to modify our plan and trust that the creator of that detour knows the best *current* course to reach the desired destination.

Author Jordan Lee Dooley courageously described the effects of life not going as planned and walking through deep loss. She explained how God was able to use suffering to strengthen her and her marriage during a long season of anguish after multiple miscarriages. She and her husband were challenged to reconsider priorities and accordingly make changes to their lifestyle. They had to learn ways to live life fully, trying new hobbies and professional endeavors, instead of just waiting around for the family life they had always envisioned. They learned to love and support each other through thick and thin while relying on their faith. "We had to learn to trust God, period. Not trust him for an outcome we wanted, but trust him regardless of the outcome."[4]

Unfortunate or disheartening events or detours in life can also be seen as opportunities to shift, learn, and grow. If we are determined to reach the desired goal despite situations not going as planned, we can learn to trust our Creator to show us an alternate route, a better *current* course. Yes, we may experience the initial sorrow or frustration that encountering an obstacle brings, but we don't have to give in to defeat. And as we move forward on the other path, we can gain confidence in new ways and learn resiliency.

In the book of Deuteronomy (31:6), Moses realizes that he, the leader who brought his people out of slavery from Egypt, is too old to continue to guide them into the Promised Land. The needed detour will require trusting a new leader to steer them past enemies and see them through to the goal. It will necessitate a shift in perspective and a willingness to proceed in this new direction to which God is calling them. Moses encourages them to "be strong and courageous. Do not be afraid or terrified because of them, for the Lord, your God, goes with you; he will never leave, nor forsake you." And God will never leave you, either, my friend. No matter the current challenge or painful circumstance, he reassures that he is walking this detour right beside you.

Fortunately, God knows there will be times we will feel extremely discouraged. He knows we will have moments of hopelessness, days of frustration, and seasons of disappointment. We need to remember that, despite these struggles and challenges, God is faithfully loving us. He knows that sometimes the best things in life come with determination and modification.

Are you willing to take a different route? Are you willing to adjust, modify, and replan to see a dream realized, even when things aren't going your way right now? Are you ready to trust God no matter what? My hope is that you are ready to reassess, redirect, and retackle the seemingly overwhelming roadblocks in your life. Begin by intentionally calming your mind and spirit as you seek acceptance that things aren't going as planned. Whether through physical activity, mindfulness, journaling, meditation, prayer, or other methods, find ways to move through the frustration and seek potential blessings on this divergent path.

The alternate track for your life may not be immediately obvious and may require frequent readjustments as you move forward. Once you feel composed enough to look past the immediate barrier, try to dig deeply to see what worthwhile lessons may be learned through this unexpected detour. Process potential positive outcomes from the course change. Is this the Lord saying the timing isn't right or that you need to make a different decision altogether? Pray for clarity and wisdom in understanding the reason your hopes and efforts have been halted. And don't be afraid to attempt the alternate route or abandon the course entirely if that is the guidance you have received from your prayers.

It takes practice to fight against the tendency to give up instead of leaning into the unexpected and going with the flow of life's circumstances. Your willingness to accept the challenge—no matter how painful—shift gears, seek alternatives, and set out on another route will determine your ultimate ability to triumph. In fact, we are often better prepared for our future when we develop those skills. Strengthening your resiliency despite disappointment provides a valuable skill that can be utilized in many areas of life.

In 2 Corinthians 4:17, the Bible reminds us that problems are momentary, and these tribulations should not make us take our eyes off the prize of eternal glory with our heavenly Father. While we may experience God on the hilltops of life, it is in the valleys where we truly come to know him. He provides strength and offers hope through the difficult times, which allows us to be better prepared for any future challenges. The next time we face a similar difficulty, setback, or roadblock, we can use the lessons learned from the current one to guide us through more easily.

It can be helpful to take encouragement from others who have also experienced discouragement when life hasn't gone as planned but have come to the other side with a new perspective. Having traveled the unplanned detour in her life, Dooley can now see God's powerful work through that difficult season. Raising an infant and pregnant with a child, she and her husband are astounded by God's goodness and double blessing. "So, if you're walking through a valley, just know it's not for nothing. Hold on to the hope that it's not a punishment—it's a privilege and a preparation for what God has called you to. Keep walking. Be steadfast. The wilderness won't last forever—but the character it creates in you will."[4] Despite the unplanned, unhoped, or unexpected, the heavenly Father will lovingly guide you to a course of greater strength and higher purpose.

So don't give up, my friend, and don't give in. Acknowledge that unplanned detours are a sometimes frustrating part of the journey. It is normal and expected to feel a cascade of emotions during this season. But also allow yourself to recognize that the diversion can improve your overall perspective and God's ultimate design for your life.

Author Susan Gesell encourages, "In hard times we learn three things—we are stronger than we ever imagined, Jesus is closer than we ever realized, and we are loved more than we ever knew." Stay the course while praying for guidance, wisdom, and strength. Take the detour and trust. Be open to accepting the changes and growth you may be experiencing on this alternate track. And then see what exciting and unexpected direction God, your Detour Creator, with a perfect path in mind, may take you.

VERSES TO ENCOURAGE YOU

"For I know the plans I have for you," declares the Lord, "plans to prosper you and not to harm you, plans to give you hope and a future."
—Jeremiah 29:11 (NIV)

The Lord hears his people when they call to him for help. He rescues them from all their troubles.
—Psalm 34:17

And we know that in all things God works for the good of those who love him, who have been called according to his purpose.
—Romans 8:28

That's why I take pleasure in my weaknesses, and in the insults, hardships, persecutions, and troubles that I suffer for Christ. For when I am weak, then I am strong.
—2 Corinthians 12:10

For I can do everything through Christ, who gives me strength.

—Philippians 4:13

SONGS FOR YOUR SOUL

- "God Is in This Story" by Katy Nichole and Big Daddy Weave
- "Whatever May Come" by Jeremy and Adrienne Camp
- "Brighter Days" by Blessing Offor
- "Hills and Valleys" by Tauren Wells

A CONVERSATION WITH GOD

Dear God,

I am feeling overwhelmed and discouraged. I thought I knew the path ahead of me, but now so much has changed. Please heal my wounds of disappointment and give me your strength in this season of weakness, uncertainty, and pain. Grant me the serenity to accept the things I cannot change, the courage to change the things I can, and the wisdom to know the difference. Give me the grace to move forward one step at a time and fill me with your peace that surpasses all understanding in the process. In Jesus's name, amen.

NOTES

CHAPTER 25

When You Need to Encourage Others

So, encourage each other and build each other up, just as
you are already doing.
                    —1 THESSALONIANS 5:11

W hen you are feeling down or discouraged in life, what do you do to overcome the slump? Is there a person in your life who can consistently lift your spirits? If so, what about this person draws you in their direction when you are feeling low? It's important for all of us to have someone affirming in our lives, and what a blessing it is to be able to fill that role for others.

Being an encourager, also known as the gift of exhortation, is one of the spiritual gifts. The Greek word in original biblical manuscripts for *exhortation* is *parakaleo*, which means "to call or come alongside." It can also be translated to mean "comfort, console, counsel, urge, appeal and encourage."[1] While this gift comes naturally for some people, we can all learn to be an encourager.

It can be easy to get caught up in our own whirlwind of busyness and neglect to notice those around us who may be hurting. It takes intentionality to not only perceive another's insecurity but also sacrifice time to reach out when they need encouragement. Numerous verses of scripture speak to the importance of lifting others emotionally and spiritually: "So, encourage each other and build each other up, just as you are already doing" (1 Thess. 5:11).

Think about that person in your life who encourages you when you are in a funk. Now try to understand what about them and your conversations with them causes you to reach out to them. Perhaps they are just in tune to your spirit and know when you need that affirming voice. There are many characteristics of good encouragers, and by utilizing these qualities, you, too, can be that positive light for others.

First, encouragers are good and empathetic listeners. They attentively hear the heart of a hurting person, seeking to truly understand their situation and concerns. Making eye contact and asking questions brings authenticity to conversations and prompts further sharing. Listening without interrupting requires patience and restraint, yet it builds trust. Trustworthiness is often valued above all else in these private conversations.

Second, encouragers have an authentic love for others that draws people to them. We not only feel heard when talking with them but also believe they truly care about us and our situation. Sharing our heart and problems with them feels safe. They don't judge us, and we don't feel shamed by them.

Great encouragers can see possible positive outcomes and instill confidence in us to work toward our goals. They invest generously in others with their time, love, guidance, resources, and positive attitude. Exploring various possible modes of action and brainstorming with us, they help us feel invested in the process. They have the ability to see our potential and help us create the self-confidence to succeed.

Being able to communicate with a positive perspective while providing an optimistic outlook is another quality of effective exhortation. When we are discouraged, we often need to hear a viewpoint that helps us believe we truly can alter the path ahead. Through wise counsel, they can suggest specific steps toward a positive outcome. The encourager can help us see the silver lining in a difficult situation and provide hope for a better future.

Great encouragers are strong advocates. In a society that often depersonalizes people, they acknowledge our worth, significance, and value as human beings. They don't try to shape us into their mold but rather see us for our individual ability to contribute to the world with our own God-given talents. By helping us understand our gifts, they encourage us to see how our talents can make a difference. When we have a misstep, we can return to them for grace, further coaching, and a revision of our plan. Seeing us for who we are, these generous advocates can motivate us to work toward our full potential.

Successful encouragers set a positive example of humility, kindness, trustworthiness, gratefulness, and respect. They are authentic in life, willing to be vulnerable and admit to their shortcomings while sharing what they have learned from their own failures. They are kind and compassionate, never using negative pressure to motivate. Because they are trustworthy, we know that our confidences will not be broken, nor will our discussion be shared with others. They often live life with an approach of gratitude and can help us see the many things in our own lives for which we can be thankful.

Finally, an effective encourager is always respectful of our hearts, our vulnerabilities, and our self-esteem. They are considerate of our feelings and seek to provide thoughtful and helpful advice. We often leave a conversation with them feeling uplifted, positive, energized, or hopeful—or all these things.

You may be thinking, *I'm not sure I can offer great advice or that my being there will truly make a meaningful difference.* But it is not chance that you are in the right place at the right time to uplift another in their hesitations or to compel them to move forward in a positive direction. Your prior experiences being on the receiving end of encouragement, combined with utilizing the above techniques of effective encouragers, create within you the intellectual and emotional foundation to make a colossal difference for someone else.

Jesus is a phenomenal Encourager. There are many examples in the Bible of his kind, compassionate, and wise counsel. Some of my favorites are the woman at the well (John 4:4–29); the calling of Levi, known as Matthew (Mark 2:13–17); and the woman caught in adultery (John 8:3–11). While Jesus has helped each of them recognize the errors of their ways, he has not berated them. He has shown love to those who have been marginalized by society, giving grace and providing hope for their futures. Jesus has delivered a wonderful example for each of us to pursue in encouraging others. And in following his example, we, too, can be great advocates for someone else.

Author Paul Tripp beautifully describes biblical encouragement that leads to lasting change because isn't that the ultimate goal? It is "about helping people see Christ with the eyes of their heart." It helps them look for the presence of Christ in their lives, the promises of Christ, and their potential in Christ.[2] Walking alongside people in their personal and faith journeys is a wonderful way to offer healing and hope.

As with everything else in life, you will become a better encourager by not only understanding what to do but also actually doing it. So when you see someone doing something positive, acknowledge it. When you have a kind thought about someone, share it. Practice on family members to gain experience and confidence. It's a win-win situation as you lift their spirits and increase your confidence in edifying others.

Motivational author William Arthur Ward tells of the effects of encouraging others in his well-known quote "Flatter me, and I may not believe you. Criticize me, and I may not like you. Ignore me, and I may not forgive you. *Encourage me*, and I will not forget you. Love me, and I may be forced to love." We have unique opportunities to interact with a variety of people daily, and we choose what tone or value to bring to those conversations. Using these moments to encourage others is a beautiful way to love people to Jesus.

Whatever is creating your hesitation to be a positive light for someone, put it aside. Those negative thoughts are not of God, friend. Stepping outside your comfort zone to be an active encourager can be life changing for them and for you. Look to the perfector of our faith as an example. Look to Jesus as your guide and then pray for the Holy Spirit to fill you with the energy, patience, compassion, humility, and words to encourage that friend in need.

VERSES TO ENCOURAGE YOU

Let us think of ways to motivate one another to acts of love and good works. And let us not neglect our meeting together, as some people do, but encourage one another, especially now that the day of his return is drawing near.
—Hebrews 10:24–25

Don't be afraid, for I am with you. Don't be discouraged, for I am your God. I will strengthen you and help you. I will hold you up with my victorious right hand.
—Isaiah 41:10

Worry weighs a person down; an encouraging word cheers a person up.
—Proverbs 12:25

Then Judas and Silas, both being prophets, spoke at length to the believers, encouraging and strengthening their faith.
—Acts 15:32

SONGS FOR YOUR SOUL

- "Fighting for Me" by Riley Clemmons
- "Something in the Water" by Carrie Underwood
- "I Will Follow" by Chris Tomlin

A CONVERSATION WITH GOD

Dear God,

Thank you for providing people in my life who have been able to encourage me during uncertain or difficult times. Thank you for being the God who loves unconditionally, restores, and brings peace. Empower me to be that gift of encouragement for someone else. Give me the wisdom, courage, and humility to lift _____ right now. Help me be your light shining into their darkness and to bring them help and hope through you. Amen.

NOTES

CHAPTER 26

When You Feel Sad or Are in Despair

The Lord is close to the brokenhearted; he rescues those
whose spirits are crushed.

—PSALM 34:18

Having lost both parents to cancer, I can still recall my feelings of hopelessness and helplessness when the diagnoses were made. Having been able to give advice for basic medical concerns or problems in many areas, cancer is wholly outside my field of expertise. Saddened by the fact that, though a trained healer, this was beyond my control, I began to fall into a state of despair. Watching the disease and treatments ravage their once healthy bodies was, at times, excruciating. If you have lost a close friend or family member to cancer, you can likely relate. And it's unfathomable to imagine how those who have lost a child or spouse to an accident or illness feel unless you have been there.

Richard Powers's novel *Bewilderment* states, "Grief is the world stripped of something you admire" or love.[1] These tragedies that strip love and beauty from our lives can create a sense of desperation, throwing us into a tailspin. Whether it's the loss of a loved one, a job, or a relationship; the terrible consequence of a poor decision; or a financial devastation, we all face moments of grief that can lead to despair. We may wonder, *Where is God? How can he let this happen?* Some may even begin to doubt their faith and the existence of God during such painful times.

I am so sorry that you are experiencing such deep sadness. It is not only OK but also healthy to allow time for processing the events that have led to your anguish. You may be finding it challenging to be around other people, which is also a normal response. Sometimes well-meaning people try to raise spirits by bringing toxic positivity to a conversation when all we really want is for someone to listen to our truth and our pain.

It is in these moments of despair that we most need our heavenly Father. When others may be either uncomfortable consoling us or too helpful in offering advice, God, who knows exactly what we need in those times, is right beside us, offering his strength and support: "The Lord is close to the brokenhearted; he rescues those whose spirits are crushed" (Ps. 34:18). When we allow ourselves to be held by our all-powerful God, he comforts and sustains us. Even when we feel we can't go on, he brings strength and hope to our situation.

Despair is a feeling of hopelessness, recognizing that things are profoundly wrong and giving in to the belief that they will never improve. It may feel like being in a long, dark tunnel with no sign of light ahead. A downward spiral of emotions can lead to severe depression and even suicidal thoughts. When those depths have been reached, it is imperative for us to seek help.

While depression is considered a multifaceted problem, science has shown an imbalance of neurotransmitters—chemicals in the brain—in people experiencing depression. Low levels of serotonin, dopamine, and norepinephrine seem to be the most relevant.[2] Serotonin, or the "feel good" hormone, not only is important in mood but also affects sleeping, eating, digestion, and sexual function. Dopamine works as a motivator because it creates positive feelings during certain tasks or activities. While too little norepinephrine in the brain seems to promote depression, too much can lead to mania. The interplay of these three neurotransmitters is complex and unique to each person.

Because these substances cannot reliably be measured on an ongoing basis, much more research is needed about these and other neurochemicals and their effects on mood. Fortunately, many people have found benefit with prescription medications that help restore a better balance of the neurotransmitters. Not everyone responds to the same medications, however, so it can take time for physicians to determine the best ones and best doses for each person.

Not everyone in a season of despair needs prescription medications for healing, but don't feel disconcerted if you do. Some find hope through talking with others, practicing yoga, doing a physical activity, or praying. These activities can enhance the release of endorphins and dopamine into the body. Others gain peace through spending time in nature or snuggling with a loved pet, which increases dopamine and oxytocin. The adjunct of psychotherapy has also been invaluable for many people.

When we feel low, depressed, or in a funk, God's heart hurts for us. He desires for us to be fulfilled and feel whole. Jesus's promise that he will always be with us (Matt. 28:20) can bring hope during these dark times in life. A great poem by Mary Stevenson reminds us of God's willingness to help us bear our burdens. Called "Footprints in the Sand," she describes a dream envisioning several of her life experiences. During many periods, there were two sets of footprints in the sand, indicating God was walking beside her. Yet during times of challenge and tribulation, she saw only one set of footprints and questioned his decision to abandon her at such difficult moments.

"Why, when I needed you most, have you not been there for me?"

The Lord replied,

"My precious child, I love you and would never leave you. During the times of trial and suffering, when you have seen only one set of footprints, it was then that I carried you."

Sit with that for a moment. Jesus carries us and our burdens when we are at our lowest points. Returning to this poem in times of despair can bring much-needed hope through the reminder that God loves us dearly and wants nothing more than to ease our pain. For some of us, it takes feeling that the bottom of the abyss has been reached before looking to our faithful God. But he is there anyway, carrying us, with our weighty worries and woes, toward his light.

Let the truth of these words wash over you and understand that you are *never* alone. Friend, it pains me to think of the depth of your current sorrow. Know that it is OK, and necessary, to take time to grieve. As you process through this season, understand that there *is* a light at the end of that long, dark tunnel. That light is the love of Jesus Christ. He has come to an earth full of broken and hurting people to save the world from hopelessness and to bring light back where there has been only darkness. He wants to shine his light on you too, but you need to ask.

God wants to hear about your fears, your frustrations, and your despair. He will not shame you nor make you feel guilty for crying out about the reality of your pain. In fact, he wants you to do just that. Once you allow God into your life, you will find help to lift and carry your burdens, any of those things that are weighing heavily on your heart. Give yourself permission to mourn. Then open your heart to God's love and assurances today. Pray for your heavenly Father to show you his compassionate faithfulness and to bring healing, then surrender your sorrows and pain to him. Trust that he *will* carry you, bringing you to that light at the end of your dark tunnel.

VERSES TO ENCOURAGE YOU

Praise the Lord; praise God our Savior! For each day he carries us in his arms.
—Psalm 68:19

Your sun will never set; your moon will not go down. For the Lord will be your everlasting light. Your days of mourning will come to an end.
—Isaiah 60:20

God blesses those who mourn, for they will be comforted.

—Matthew 5:4

I cried out to the Lord in my great trouble, and he answered me.

—Jonah 2:2

SONGS FOR YOUR SOUL

- "I Will Carry You" by Ellie Holcomb
- "By Your Side" by Tenth Avenue North
- "Scars" by I Am They
- "Don't Lose Heart" by Steven Curtis Chapman

A CONVERSATION WITH GOD

Dear God,

I feel so helpless right now. I know you have guided me through hard times in the past, yet this seems insurmountable. Father, hear my cries for help. Fill me with your Spirit and give me the strength to continue forward. Carry me through this burden and give me the comfort and peace I need to see your hope on the other side. Help me see your light, Jesus. Amen.

NOTES

CHAPTER 27

When You Are Tempted to Judge Others

Do to others as you would like them to do to you.
—LUKE 6:31

I njustice is to judge a person unfairly. We have learned biases, often unrecognized, that can direct our thoughts, words, and actions. These tendencies to think a certain way, which deviate from rationality or good judgment, ultimately lead to unintentional or intentional discrimination. Author Alaric Hutchinson warns, "Your judgments about another person say more about your own character than the character of the person you are pointing a finger at."[1]

We can see how this type of cognitive bias has led to local, national, and global tragedies. It is disturbing and heartbreaking to see or hear about the victims of unfair judgment or discrimination in the news. Yet people tend to assess others daily, often without even realizing it. We perceive our judgments as reality, frequently without considering any other perspectives.

If you are recognizing some tendencies to judge others, you are not alone. As we try harder and harder to become more successful, it almost seems natural to make subjective assessments about other people along the way. It takes great effort and dedication to loving others well to shatter the societal norms of comparing ourselves with and making judgments about others. Take heart, my friend, that making this change in perceptions and attitude is absolutely possible and within your grasp.

When we make rash or undeserved assessments of another person, our biased thoughts can lead to harmful words or behaviors. When we share our judgment with other people, who then may share this with someone else, we see how these biases can spiral out of control. Jesus has spoken to his disciples about a better choice: "Do to others as you would like them to do to you" (Luke 6:31). In other words, if we don't want people to judge us by our faults and imperfections, of which we all have many, we should refrain from judging them.

How can we recognize when we are being judgmental, and what causes us to form these biases? Rubin Khoddam, PhD, a clinical psychologist and founder of COPE Psychological Center in Los Angeles, describes the process of fusion when people make judgments. In arguments, we tend to *fuse* with our opinions. Khoddam states, "We fuse, meaning that we can't tell the difference between what our opinion is and what the reality is. And in the end, our perception becomes our reality. However, this is not a universal reality. We end up believing our thoughts/judgments, and take our thoughts as reality."[2]

In fusion, we see people and situations through our personal lens, which we then accept as fact or truth. We fail to recognize the possibility that these judgments may be the result of individual bias or judgment. This also creates a lack of acceptance of other people's beliefs and a feeling of superiority.

People who are judged often feel ashamed, humiliated, misunderstood, frustrated, criticized, and dejected. These emotions lead to loneliness and isolation. In some cases, the one who is judged becomes depressed and retreats, while in others, the victim becomes frustrated and lashes out. Although we may not intend to harm that person or others, the result of our judgments is to create a negative energy and the potential for devastating outcomes.

When expressing our opinions, it is possible to do so while leaving the door open to others' viewpoints. For example, saying, "That painting is ugly," states the view as fact, whereas saying, "I don't care for that painting," leaves room for others to disagree and express their perceptions. The same is true whether we are discussing somewhat trivial subjects or significant topics such as another person, political beliefs, ethnic groups, or religion.

When expressing our ideas, are we truly open to hearing and trying to understand a different view? Or are we convinced that we are right, and therefore, the other person is wrong? Do we monopolize conversations, trying to prove our points, or do we engage in healthy listening and openhearted discussions? And perhaps more importantly, are we able to love others well despite having differing opinions?

Because Jesus has modeled for us a life of perfection, we can learn from the actions he has taken. In the Gospels, we encounter a Jesus who is compassionate, forgiving, peaceful, patient, and unprejudiced and who loves unconditionally. Biblical examples of unfair judgment include a crowd wanting to stone a woman caught in adultery (John 8:1–11), a woman who was seen as a sinner washing Jesus's feet (Mark 14:3–9), and a leper who was a societal outcast (Matt. 8:1–4). In each of these examples, Jesus responds with kindness and compassion. He does not ignite nor incite but rather promotes peace.

In the book of Acts, Peter receives a vision during his prayer time that is confusing. In the vision, he is told to kill and eat animals that are not kosher according to Jewish laws. But when Peter refuses, God responds, "Do not call something unclean that God has made clean" (Acts 10:15).

After seeing the same vision three times, the Holy Spirit calls Peter to the home of a Roman officer. Although it is against Jewish law to enter the home of such a gentile, Peter has learned from his vision, God's voice, and the conviction of the Holy Spirit that those preconceived or cognitive biases do not lead to the behavior God desires of him: "But God has shown me that I should no longer think of anyone as impure or unclean" (Acts 10:28).

We must each take an honest look at our thought patterns and opinions. Where may we be exercising unfair judgment? Against what person or group of people is our spirit hardened? Are we able to open our minds and hearts to others' views, or have we decided that we are definitively right? These may not be easy questions to answer. And it is often challenging to recognize such biases in our own thought patterns. It is important to pray, therefore, for an open and malleable heart before, during, and after this type of self-reflection.

When tempted to make a quick judgment based on superficial information, we need to pause intentionally. Then we should try to view the person empathetically from their perspective, putting ourselves in their shoes. As we visualize walking through someone else's pain, we begin to recognize more similarities than polarizing differences. This provides an opportunity to practice mindfulness, calmly observing our thoughts without passing judgment on ourselves or others[3] (see appendix).

Overcoming judgmentalism is possible, and it is a testament to your openness that you have chosen to read this chapter. Pray, calmly listening and allowing the Holy Spirit to guide your thoughts. Encourage your mind to embrace new perspectives. Seek to compassionately understand people not based on how they look but for who they are. Truly digging deeply and being open to other views, ideas, beliefs, or lifestyles may not be simple, but it does allow self-enlightenment, acceptance, and growth.

God's righteous path requires us, like Peter, to no longer think of or judge anyone as inferior or unclean. Soften your heart today, friend. Willingly accept others for who they are, another of God's children. Visualize your heavenly Father standing beside the one you are tempted to judge, with his powerful hand lovingly resting on their shoulder. Then instead of passing judgment, become a vessel to pour out God's love, patience, and gentleness. Begin to bridge the gap between you and that person and pave the way to hope and healing. As others witness your admirable intentions, you may just open the gate to the better world God has intended.

VERSES TO ENCOURAGE YOU

What is important is faith expressing itself in love.
—Galatians 5:6

But the wisdom from above is first of all pure. It is also peace-loving, gentle at times, and willing to yield to others. It is full of mercy, and the fruit is good deeds.
—James 3:17

Do not judge others, and you will not be judged. For you will be treated as you treat others. The standard you use in judging is the standard by which you will be judged. And why worry about a speck in your friend's eye when you have a log in your own?

—Matthew 7:1–3

Don't speak evil against each other, dear brothers and sisters. If you criticize and judge each other, then you are criticizing and judging God's law.

—James 4:11

SONGS FOR YOUR SOUL

- "Open the Eyes of My Heart" by Michael W. Smith
- "From the Inside Out" by Hillsong United

A CONVERSATION WITH GOD

Dear God,

I realize that I am challenged by the temptation to judge other people. When comparing myself with others, I often find it hard to accept my personal gifts and blessings and instead wind up finding a reason to criticize theirs. Help me remember that each of us is created and gifted uniquely, Lord. Instead of passing judgments, help me sow seeds of acceptance, love, and grace. In Jesus's name, amen.

NOTES

CHAPTER 28

When You Are Tempted to Gossip

Those who control their tongue will have a long life;
opening your mouth can ruin everything.
— PROVERBS 13:3

W ords are potentially dangerous. Once said, they can never be taken back. Words are also capable of destroying friendships, ruining families, breaking hearts, shaking self-confidence, and destroying souls. Educator and author Stephen Covey has once asked this valid question: "Isn't it kind of silly to think that tearing someone else down builds you up?"

We have seen too many instances where comments and gossip on social media have led to psychological pain and devastating outcomes, including suicide. Gossips are often seen as uncaring, self-interested, unlikable, and untrustworthy. None of these are honorable characteristics that most of us want.

I sincerely doubt that you have malicious intentions when discussing other people. When we carelessly gossip, however, we run the risk of damaging our relationships. Is that truly what we want? We are cautioned throughout the Bible to use our voice gently and thoughtfully: "Those who control their tongue will have a long life; opening your mouth can ruin everything" (Prov. 13:3). So why do people gossip? What is the internal driving force of this common behavior?

Because we innately desire to be part of a community, gossiping gives some people a sense of belonging and connection to others. Research has shown that gossiping can actually decrease the likelihood of loneliness.[1] And not all conversations about others are malicious or negative. But it is in verbalizing rumors, criticisms, and judgments of others not present that we move into dangerous territory. Joining in the gossip creates a false and momentary sense of belonging since we may be the next unfortunate target of it when we are not present.

Some people want to be in the know to feel included, believing they are being rejected if information is kept from them. But don't we all have a right to privacy? Gossiping invades that privacy. Another reason insecure people may join in gossiping about someone else is self-protection. When the focus of the conversation is on someone else, then we know the negative attention is not directed toward us.

Others gossip because it makes them feel better about themselves. They may say, "Look at all the problems she has," or "Can you believe he did that?" or "I heard they ..." But is it really OK to humiliate someone else just to make us feel better about ourselves? How will we feel if we are the target of such gossip? And are these statements based on bias or fact? As inspirational author and therapist Shannon Alder reminds us, often those who criticize others reveal what they themselves lack.

Unfortunately, negative gossip often leads to the exaggeration of a truth or even a fabricated story. The story or mistruth grows as it is passed along and can lead to significant harm. Sadly, some people thrive on knowing what everyone else is doing and share that information openly without considering the person's feelings. It is even more damaging to the gossip victim and to relationships when the shared information is told in confidence.

The book of Proverbs is one of many in the Bible that speaks to the harmfulness of gossip. In Proverbs 25:23, we are reminded that gossip creates anger and strife, and in Proverbs 11:13, that gossip is a betrayal. We are encouraged instead to be trustworthy, an important quality in good friends. In Proverbs 16:28, we are cautioned that gossip destroys relationships. Psalm 15:3 advises us to refuse to gossip, speak evil of our friends, or harm our neighbors to live righteously.

God has made it very clear that he despises negative gossiping. Instead, he teaches us to love and build up one another. Gossip may be disguised as a friendly invitation to fellowship, but it is hurtful and destructive. Gossip has been described as divisive, poisonous, foolish, and not in God's plan for our lives. There is rarely a mutually beneficial result from negative conversations about others.

When we find ourselves in a situation in which people are gossiping, we have the choice of whether to join in. We may think, *They are already talking about her, so what can it hurt?* However, rationalization doesn't promote a positive outcome. It takes intentionality in our thoughts and words to shift the focus from conversational gossip and the potential negative impact.

Next time you face this choice to join a gossip-filled chat, stop. Ask yourself three questions about the conversation before joining in:

1. Is it true?
2. Is it helpful?
3. Is it kind?

If the answer to any of those questions is no, then I encourage you to either shift the conversation in another direction or to walk away. While it may be difficult initially not to join in negative gossip, taking this approach becomes easier with practice. Choosing not to participate can increase your sense of self-worth and your value as a true and trustworthy friend.

Another approach is to stop negativity before it can start. When in conversation, be intentional to say something constructive about others. Become the encourager others seek out because of your affirming energy. Shift any negative gossip in a different direction. Focus on being kind and gentle, respecting others with your words. Can you imagine the positive impact you will make? I can visualize God smiling as you use your words to empower others. Choose to follow Jesus's example and radiate the love that the heavenly Father pours into you. Then watch it overflow as a river of encouragement to others.

VERSES TO ENCOURAGE YOU

Let everything you say be good and helpful, so that your words will be an encouragement to those who hear them.

—Ephesians 4:29

Do not spread slanderous gossip among your people.

—Leviticus 19:16

A gossip goes around telling secrets, but those who are trustworthy can keep a confidence.

—Proverbs 11:13

If you claim to be religious but don't control your tongue, you are fooling yourself, and your religion is worthless.

—James 1:26

SONGS FOR YOUR SOUL

- "If We Are the Body" by Casting Crowns
- "Stay Strong" by Newsboys

A CONVERSATION WITH GOD

Dear God,

As I engage with others, help me be mindful of my words. When the conversation turns to negativity and gossip, Lord, give me the courage to defuse and redirect it. Help me be the friend whom others can trust with their confidences and be a vessel of your love and kindness. In Jesus's name, amen.

NOTES

CHAPTER 29

When You Are Called to Be a Leader

Don't be selfish; don't try to impress others. Be humble, thinking of others as better than yourselves.

—PHILIPPIANS 2:3

Congratulations! You have been asked to be a leader. Whether at work, at home, in church, or in the community, others have been entrusted to your guidance and influence. Taking on a position of leadership may feel gratifying and exciting and at the same time daunting and terrifying. This role brings not only responsibility but also great opportunity. Pastor and author John C. Maxwell says, "A leader is one who knows the way, goes the way, and shows the way." How you develop your role as a leader has the potential to affect many people and ultimately God's kingdom.

Numerous books have been written on leadership, so attacking the topic in a short chapter is challenging. Use this as a quick resource to begin your journey. But don't stop here. Continuing to learn, grow, and improve while adapting to situations at hand is the sign of a great leader. And don't try to go it alone if this is a new position. Reaching out to others in leadership roles for advice is often both educational and encouraging.

Have you considered why you have been asked to lead this endeavor? Do you feel God's hand in opening your heart to accepting the position?

The Bible is filled with wise words to encourage you through this process. It also provides counsel for potentially destructive behaviors and encourages generous leadership: "Don't be selfish; don't try to impress others. Be humble, thinking of others as better than yourselves" (Phil. 2:3). Following these pieces of wisdom and trusting God through the leadership process increases your likelihood of success.

Strong leaders exhibit mutually beneficial qualities and strategies in their position that are shown to increase the likelihood of team success. Brian Eastwood, an educator on leadership strategies, says there are five characteristics common among all successful leaders: being self-aware while prioritizing personal development, concentrating on developing others, encouraging strategic thinking and innovation, making ethical decisions, and being an effective communicator.[1]

Having the ability to recognize their own strengths and weaknesses, as well as those of each team member, is an important aspect of being a successful leader. While some refrain from revealing any personal shortcomings, an effective leader is authentic and accepting of the fact that other team members are better suited to certain tasks than they are. These leaders, who are genuine in words and actions, breed a culture of mutual trust.

Encouraging team members to learn and grow continually as individuals stimulates an environment for personal and ultimately team development. Strong leaders are passionate visionaries. Acknowledging colleagues' inventive thoughts and acting on them encourages others on the team to think outside the box. Seeing the potential for new, innovative outcomes, they courageously inspire team members to enhance their vision while motivating everyone to take the necessary steps to reach their common goal with passionate purpose.

Clear communication to the unit as a whole, as well as providing individual feedback, keeps the project moving forward. Ineffective communicators often have teams that are disorganized and resort to unproductive measures such as duplicate work. Lack of communication can lead to misunderstanding, angst, and hostility. Clear and effective communication, on the other hand, creates an atmosphere of optimal teamwork and is the backbone of any successful group.

Because many people are resistant to venturing beyond their comfort zones, it is the responsibility of an effective leader to challenge the group to grow. Some of the attempts to head in a new direction will likely fail, which can be uncomfortable. Pain and growth, however, often go hand in hand. Providing reassurance beyond the failed attempts allows further team-building opportunities. Taking the group in a new direction is not without risks, but once the goal has been achieved, the final reward is worth the gamble.

As the group relies on the head for guidance and direction, they must find their leader to be honest. Modeling honesty and integrity helps create a team that is trustworthy in their efforts. In his book *The Healing Organization*, author Raj Sisodia describes successful organizations with loyal participants in which the leader encourages a culture of "fairness, truth, beauty, integrity, and basic goodness."[2] By providing ethical leadership team members can depend on, a leader enables the group to learn to trust one another, building a culture of loyalty.

Excellent leadership includes the following strategies: communication, delegation, collaboration, and acclimation. Clear communication begins with detailing the group's goals, ascertaining that everyone is on the same page from the start. Listening honestly and openly to feedback and then acting on it promotes a feeling of comradery, breeds a team culture, and delivers the greatest chance of success.

Delegating responsibilities based on knowledge and expertise is a critical stage that allows everyone in the group to bring value in achieving the desired result. Implementing the team approach, in which each individual's contribution is necessary to the success of the whole group, creates an atmosphere of shared respect and a model of humility for the team to follow. This positive attitude helps members of the group understand that the greatest accomplishments are achieved through a collaborative environment, which is beneficial as the team members partner toward mutual growth.

Great leaders have the ability to acclimate throughout the process and help their teams do the same. While it's easy to always do things the same way, especially when it has once been successful, this stifles creativity, initiative, and the opportunity for improvement. If the group seems to have gotten into a rut, the leader may gently remind them that improvement is accomplished only if there is a willingness to change.

Finally, the best and most effective leaders guide with a servant's heart. They are willing to sacrifice their own recognition and pride to better serve their team members. Selfless toughness is required, which means taking a back seat to benefit others and the cause they passionately serve. Great servant leaders feel most rewarded not in their own accomplishments but in the achievements of their team members as they collectively pursue the purpose with passion. Alan Major, a renowned basketball coach at the University of North Carolina–Charlotte and other universities, declares, "The fruit of a good leader grows on other people's trees." Selflessly serving the greater purpose and the team generates a path to tall and fruitful trees.

Jesus provides the perfect model of sacrificial servant leadership. In John 13:1–17, nearing the time of his death and after three years of teaching, guiding, and rebuking his dear friends, Jesus washes the disciples' filthy, mud-caked feet in a gesture of humility and love. Horrified to see his Teacher and Lord preparing to wash his feet, Peter protests, "You will never wash my feet!" Yet Jesus reassures Peter it is a necessary step in their bond in fully allowing him into their hearts.

After washing the feet of all twelve followers, even the disciple he knows will betray him, Jesus says to them, "And since I, your Lord and Teacher, have washed your feet, you ought to wash each other's feet. I have given you an example to follow. Do as I have done to you" (John 13:14–15). Jesus is a humble, gentle, visionary leader with passion for his purpose. His success is evident in the number of Christian believers who exist worldwide over two thousand years later.

Friend, take heart. You are not in this role by accident. God has a divine purpose in your position of leadership. Pray for his direction as you lead and never stop pursuing everything you are meant to be. Pray through team challenges. Humbly follow his guidance while listening to and attentively serving your team and the purpose. Create a collaborative environment with a passionate heart. Trust the Lord in your doubts and relinquish any need for recognition. Allow the power of the Holy Spirit to wash over you with a waterfall of purpose and peace as you forge ahead. Your selfless enthusiasm will pave the way for a bountiful yield of fruit beyond what you can imagine or even hope for.

VERSES TO ENCOURAGE YOU

Now all glory to God, who is able, through his mighty power at work within us, to accomplish infinitely more than we might ask or think.

—Ephesians 3:20

Whoever wants to be a leader among you must be your servant, and whoever wants to be first among you must be the slave of everyone else. For even the Son of Man came not to be served but to serve others and to give his life as a ransom for many.

—Mark 10:43–45

Commit your actions to the Lord, and your plans will succeed.

—Proverbs 16:3

I will instruct you and teach you the way you should go; I will counsel you with my loving eye on you.

—Psalm 32:8 (NIV)

SONGS FOR YOUR SOUL

- "Rise Up (Lazarus)" by CAIN
- "Confidence" by Sanctus Real

A CONVERSATION WITH GOD

Dear God,

Yikes! I am excited yet nervous to lead. This opportunity has the potential to bring so much reward, but there are sure to be challenges along the way. Give me your wisdom and guidance through each step, Lord. Open my mind to others' ideas and perspectives. Give me an ongoing passion for the purpose and the ability to remain focused on the goal. Help me serve humbly and selflessly so that I may glorify you. In Jesus's name, amen.

NOTES

CHAPTER 30

When You Want to Be Generous or Serve Others

> Wherever your treasure is, there the desires of your heart will also be.
>
> —MATTHEW 6:21

We live in a world full of people who are hurting, vulnerable, and in need. Yet we also live in a society that defines success through accumulation of wealth, power, and possessions. Poet Kahlil Gibran has said, "Generosity is not giving me that which I need more than you do, but it is giving me that which you need more than I do." Being generous, then, requires us to become comfortable with the prospect of giving away something we believe we either need now or may need in the future.

Am I being irresponsible in my retirement planning when I donate financial resources to charitable causes? Am I putting my family at risk when, despite limited income, I give regularly to my local church? What if the commitments to helping others are taking away from my family time? What does it take to become a person who is generous with their time, talents, and resources without being reckless? Many of us struggle with these and other issues surrounding generosity.

I love that you have opened to this chapter, and I understand the initial risk it takes to be generous. Being openhanded and willing to give of yourself or your financial resources may seem easy on the surface, and the thought can be exciting. But once we prepare to make the commitment, underlying uncertainties may emerge and cause us to question the wisdom in moving forward. If this is where you find yourself, don't feel guilty and don't be discouraged. This is a common part of the process of becoming dedicatedly benevolent.

We may say, "After I have paid off all my debts, I will give to charity," or "Once I have enough for the down payment on my house, I'll give to the church," or "I will start to volunteer my time when my kids are fully grown and out of the house," or perhaps, "When I have time left over from work, social activities, Bible studies, and self-care, then I will give my time to other causes." You can probably insert several reasons or excuses of your own. Yet isn't there a part of you yearning to give more or do more right now to make a difference?

Scripture encourages us to be generous, giving to those who are in need physically, mentally, or spiritually. We are asked to look beyond our personal needs and open our hearts to the possibility of sharing to ease another's pain. Where we put our resources of time, energy, and finances speaks to our character: "Wherever your treasure is, there the desires of your heart will also be" (Matt. 6:21). In looking outward instead of inward, we open our eyes to the reality of the immense pain and human need surrounding us. Imagine being the life-changing vessel in someone else's difficult journey. Imagine the impact your generosity may have and the opportunities it may create.

According to the Science of Generosity initiative at the University of Notre Dame, *generosity* is defined as "giving good things to others freely and abundantly."[1] What is our motivation to give? Through an accumulation of multiple studies, science has shown that, over time, humans have become more generous to one another. This fact is attributed to the evolution toward the survival of the species.

Giving also generates a feeling of pleasure or joy. Neuroscientist Jordan Grafman, PhD, and colleagues have used specialized brain scans to discover that the midbrain shows increased blood flow when study subjects engage in generous acts. This same neurologic reward pathway is triggered by other pleasurable activities, such as sex and food.[2] Through this mesolimbic pathway, endorphins, such as oxytocin, are released when we help someone. Thus, we are literally physiologically wired to be altruistic.

There are also many health benefits to generosity. Various studies have shown benevolence to be related to lower blood pressure and stress levels, increased self-esteem, longer life span, decreased incidence of depression, and overall greater happiness and satisfaction in life.[3, 4] All these factors show that it not only feels good but also *is* good, and healthier, to be generous.

But these scientific facts don't account for the reality of life with its financial challenges and time demands. How do we practically achieve the balance of being fiscally responsible and charitable? How can we realistically volunteer time to worthy causes without creating burnout? The answer comes in prioritization.

If we always put donating time and resources at the bottom of our list, after everything else has been done or paid for, then we will rarely find the time or funds to be generous. Instead, we need to be intentional about scheduling the time to volunteer before filling our social calendars. We need to be deliberate about setting aside the percent of our income we wish to donate before paying other expenses. It is amazing to see how, when we truly prioritize generosity, God redeems our time and cares for all our financial needs.

Giving selflessly to others is what Jesus has modeled and taught: "It is more blessed to give than to receive" (Acts 20:35). Jesus has shown us countless acts of generosity in giving his love, time, and resources. Whenever he faces someone in need, Jesus has not only fulfilled that need but also often given more than they have asked or hoped for. And we have the capacity to make that same difference when we encounter human need by practicing charity.

In the Old Testament book of Malachi, we are even challenged to test God through our generosity: "'Bring all the tithes into the storehouse so there will be enough food in my Temple. If you do,' says the Lord of Heaven's Armies, 'I will open the windows of heaven for you. I will pour out a blessing so great, you won't have enough room to take it in! Try it! Put me to the test!'" (3:10). That particular challenge, to be charitable with abandon, is both inspiring and motivating.

Finally, we are encouraged in 2 Corinthians to not give begrudgingly of our time, talents, and resources out of frustrated obligation or in response to pressure. Rather, we are to give generously from our softened hearts in response to human need. When we see a need with softened hearts, our immediate response is to provide. God loves when we give freely and joyfully.

"We make a living by what we get; we make a life by what we give." Reading that adage for the first time gave my husband and me pause. Were we simply working to make a living, to support our family and provide life's necessities and pleasures? Or were we intentionally giving to make a life and create better lives for others? While feeling we had been generous, after intentional reflecting, we knew we could do more. This realization was a potent motivator that challenged us to seek additional opportunities for sharing our gifts and talents. In our quest for generosity, we made two practical changes that might help you in your own pursuit.

First, prioritize financial giving by placing it at the top of the list, even before mortgage, rent, or food. This likely seems scary. It requires surrendering your finances to the Lord and trusting that he will come through when you need it. Yet we have seen time and again, and heard many stories from other families, how God blesses that faithful choice by assuring we have what we need.

Second, ponder and accept the truth that all your blessings, financial and otherwise, are from God. He is a lavish and loving Father who allows you to keep 90 percent of the abundant blessing he gives. God only asks that his followers give back 10 percent (Lev. 27:30). When considering that perspective, being generous is a bit less intimidating.

You may not be ready to give a full biblical 10 percent tithe, and that is OK! Perhaps begin by challenging yourself to increase financial charitable giving by 2 percent this year. In setting aside that amount regularly, you will find that you can actually make do with less. Once comfortable with that amount, perhaps increase it by 1 to 2 percent a year until you reach the amount that your heart is calling you to give.

Donating funds may mean skipping a fancy morning coffee, dining out one less time a month, or having one fewer article of new clothing. But are those things truly necessary to our survival? As we imagine donating those funds to someone whose survival truly does depend on them, we gain a healthy perspective on the conflict of wants versus needs. It can help each of us look beyond the focus on our small world to the vast atmosphere of need all around us.

Because you have chosen this chapter, your heart is likely calling you to increase your generosity. What is holding you back from making a life with the best parts of you? Pray over those obstacles and ask God to soften your spirit and show you the way. Pray for him to give you peace as you trust him in this area that challenges so many of us. Sacrificing time and giving of your resources to make a difference in the world around you is the beginning of creating a rich and fulfilling life.

Explore the passions of your heart today. Where are you feeling fervently nudged to give of your time, talents, and resources? Take time to purposefully pray over the ways in which you can contribute to the betterment of God's kingdom in this area. Once a path becomes clear, don't delay, my friend. Start small but dream big. Accept God's challenge to put him to the test in generosity. And then watch him impress and bless you beyond what you may imagine.

VERSES TO ENCOURAGE YOU

You must each decide in your heart how much to give. And don't give reluctantly or in response to pressure. "For God loves a person who gives cheerfully." And God will generously provide all you need. Then you will always have everything you need and plenty left over to share with others.
—2 Corinthians 9:7–8

When God's people are in need, be ready to help them.
—Romans 12:13

Oh, the joys of those who are kind to the poor! The Lord rescues them when they are in trouble.

—Psalm 41:1

The generous will prosper; those who refresh others will themselves be refreshed.

—Proverbs 11:25

SONGS FOR YOUR SOUL

- "I Refuse" by Josh Wilson
- "Send Me Out" by Fee
- "God of Justice" by Tim Hughes

A CONVERSATION WITH GOD

Dear God,

My heart wants to give back, but my head seems to get in the way. There are so many distractions, obligations, and personal financial struggles that I can easily justify not following through with the divine nudge to give generously to others. Help me look beyond myself and my own needs and truly see the greater needs in my community. Show me where and to whom you want me to dedicate my time, talents, and resources. God, give me the courage to be the hands and feet of Jesus by living a life of generosity. In his name, I pray. Amen.

# NOTES

CHAPTER 31

When Your Prayers Seem to Go Unanswered

Such things were written in the Scriptures long ago to teach us. And the Scriptures give us hope and encouragement as we wait patiently for God's promises to be fulfilled.
— ROMANS 15:4

We all can probably think of a time, or perhaps many times, when we have prayed for something important to us and felt the prayer has not been answered. The resulting disappointment can be a heartbreaking challenge to our faith. If God tells us that he loves us and wants us to bring our requests to him, why does he leave us hanging?

Maybe we have prayed for something that hasn't happened, such as the healing of a loved one or a big job promotion. Singer Garth Brooks once said, "Some of God's greatest gifts are unanswered prayers." An unanswered prayer now may be paving the way to a huge blessing down the road. Yet in moments of fear, uncertainty, or anger, this seems to be far from a recognizable or desired gift. Instead, we can be left feeling defeated and hopeless. What, then, should we do with the frustration that can occur when our prayers seem to go unanswered?

First, let me acknowledge the reality and rationality of your discouragement. It is a human response to disappointment to feel this way. And when we are trying to reach out to our all-powerful God for help in an area with seemingly no response, we can begin to question the goodness of our heavenly Father. While acknowledging the validity of your pain, I also encourage you not to allow yourself to remain stuck in the depths and darkness that can result from the frustration you are feeling. Instead, when faced with the frustration of unanswered prayers, we need to try to keep an open mind to the divine possibilities that may lie ahead.

We need to begin by remembering that, while God asks us to bring all our concerns and requests to him, he does not say that he will provide for all our wishes. Rather than a magic genie in a lamp granting us whatever we want, he is a loving Father who ultimately desires what is best for us. As children of a generous and gracious God, we should have prayers that are humble requests, not narcissistic demands. And while we may believe we know what is best for us, God likely will sometimes disagree.

It's in the face of these disappointments that we need to exercise our willingness to trust the heavenly Father with our current circumstances. We must believe that his timing is perfect and that following his will always brings about what is best for us. "Such things were written in the Scriptures long ago to teach us. And the Scriptures give us hope and encouragement as we wait patiently for God's promises to be fulfilled" (Rom. 15:4). The directive to wait patiently is far from easy, especially when the prayer is for something significant that greatly affects our life's journey. It requires intentionality and a great deal of faith to remain patiently hopeful.

It may not always seem true, but God does always answer our prayers. His response may be, "No," "Slow," or "Go." It's difficult to understand why we get a no from God when asking for something very important to us, such as a life mate, a painful period to end, or the feeling of joy again. When God seems to allow sorrow in our lives, he may be trying to encourage us to grow in some way.

For many of us, the pandemic that began in 2020 brought great suffering in the form of lost jobs, lost connections to people, lost opportunities, and lost lives of friends or family. It also brought unexpected blessings. We found an opening for us to let go of unimportant things, to cherish time with family, and to reflect on anything that might be hindering our walk with the Lord. During the pandemic, people reported feeling God providing an intentional pathway toward valuable lessons: the importance of prioritizing family time, working fewer hours, appreciating health, and relishing the small things in life.

During difficult times, we must trust that God is always walking right alongside us down these and other painful pathways. In reaching the other side of the pain, we hopefully gain strength and understanding while experiencing personal growth. We may at times receive a no from God because he is answering a bigger prayer and has insight about the greater picture. While we may have prayed to get into an Ivy League college, perhaps he knows that the lifelong friendships that will be formed with godly people at the state school will be more important in the long run. Or maybe the job promotion doesn't come through because he knows that a better opportunity is around the bend. Perhaps the inability to get pregnant at a desired time is because God knows that having a child at that moment will strain the marriage during a difficult season.

In his book *Christian Reflections*, C. S. Lewis has written, "I must often be glad that certain past prayers of my own were not granted."[1] Whereas we live in the here and now, God sees a much bigger picture. He, in his infinite wisdom and knowledge of who we are through the depths of our souls, does not always provide what we seek. Trusting that he still wants what is best for us can be especially trying when God's answer to a prayer is no. Yet that is exactly what we must learn to do. When we defiantly move forward without an answer from the Lord, we set ourselves up for heartbreak, failure, and disappointment.

Sometimes it may feel as if God has vindictively refused our prayer request. Lewis offers these encouraging words: "When the opposite event occurs, your prayer has never been ignored; it has been considered and refused for your ultimate good."[2] This can be a hard and disappointing truth to swallow. Yet we need to believe that God's "no" may lead to the blessing of a bigger and better plan than we can ever have imagined.

Sometimes God's answer to our prayers is, "Slow." As impatient people, we tend to want everything here and now. Our culture is filled with instant gratification through fast food, rapid internet searches, and immediate social media connections. Yet instant responses to prayer seem to be uncommon. Whether it is because we have growing to do before receiving a yes or the timing is not quite right, we need to again trust that God alone knows the best timeline for our life events to occur. Rushing ahead without God creates the potential for complete chaos in our lives. Trusting that his timing is always perfect requires patient strength.

Fortunately, sometimes God's answer to our prayers is, "Go." The go may follow a no, giving us the opportunity to see a different path. Or the go may follow a "slow," giving us the chance to grow in some way, making the ultimate yes more meaningful or productive. While a quick yes to prayer seems infrequent, when we have trusted God despite each no and through the slow periods of growth, we can also trust his yes, urging us to move forward.

There are steps we can take when suffering the frustration of unanswered prayer. First, we can invite the Holy Spirit to help us honestly explore the motivation behind the prayer. Is the request based on a selfish desire? Is the answered prayer potentially benefiting only ourselves, or is there a component of a greater good? Perhaps adapting our prayer to a more selfless one is in order.

Second, are we aligning our prayer requests with God's will for our life? His plan for us may be very different from our current limited vision. As difficult as it may be in the moment, we must open our heart to the possibility that he has much more in store for us. We then need to spend intentional prayer time, seeking his will rather than our own.

Finally, working through disappointment from unanswered prayers takes patience. This can be difficult when living in a quick-fix society. We may fall into the habit of praying for the rapid outcome instead of the growing process. Know that there is a divine purpose in the way our prayers are answered, even if they feel unanswered in the moment. As we surrender our lives to Jesus, we learn to trust, in humility and with a childlike faith, that God's plan is better than our own.

Today as you wrestle with disappointment, rely on the truth that your heavenly Father loves you more fully than you can imagine. And through that love, your seemingly unanswered prayers take form and purpose. Friend, I pray that you let go of frustration and discouragement. Instead, focus your heart today on trusting the Creator, who knows you even better than you know yourself. His plans for you are always good, and his timing is always perfect. As difficult as it may be today, be patient and keep praying. Trust that there may just be a great gift in the waiting.

VERSES TO ENCOURAGE YOU

"For I know the plans I have for you," declares the Lord, "plans to prosper you and not to harm you, plans to give you hope and a future."
—Jeremiah 29:11 (NIV)

Rejoice in our confident hope. Be patient in trouble, and keep on praying.
—Romans 12:12

The Lord isn't really being slow about his promise. No, he is being patient for your sake.
—2 Peter 3:9

Meanwhile, the moment we get tired in the waiting, God's spirit is right alongside helping us along. If we don't know how or what to pray, it doesn't matter. He does our praying in and for us, making prayer out of our wordless sighs, our aching groans.
—Romans 8:26 (MSG)

SONGS FOR YOUR SOUL

- "Haven't Seen It Yet" by Danny Gokey
- "Plans" by Rend Collective
- "Great Is Thy Faithfulness" by Jordan Smith

A CONVERSATION WITH GOD

Dear God,

I get so discouraged when it seems you are not listening to my prayers. If I am being honest, I have also been angry when I prayed for something and the opposite happened. Lord, help me trust you when your answer to my prayer is yes and when the answer is no. Help me see your hand making a positive future for my life, even when my prayers feel like they aren't being answered. Give me the patience to trust your timing, God, knowing that you love me and want what is ultimately best for my future. I pray all this in Jesus's name. Amen.

NOTES

CHAPTER 32

When You Have Been Betrayed

Rejoice in our confident hope. Be patient in trouble, and
keep on praying.

—ROMANS 12:12

Deception, duplicity, unfaithfulness,
disloyalty, betrayal—it hurts. It's
raw. It's real. Life coach Gugu Mofokeng maintains, "Nothing hurts
more than being disappointed by the one person who you thought
would never hurt you." When betrayed by that trusted person, we are
left open and wounded. Having walked through betrayal with several
people close to me, I can easily recall the devastating effects it had on
them. I have also suffered the betrayal of a loved one, as many of us have.
The resulting hurt can be unbearable.

I am so sorry that you are suffering this pain. The wounds of
betrayal are some of the most difficult to heal, and the enemy uses
our woundedness to further his lies in our minds and lives. You may
be questioning yourself, looking for faults of your own that may have
led to the betrayal. You may also be having difficulty trusting anyone
right now. During these times of extreme vulnerability, confiding in an
empathetic friend and relying on a trustworthy God can help you move
past the pain, begin the process of healing, and regain your life.

God knows your pain. He hurts when you are hurting and wants you to feel whole again. Friend, although God loves you right where you are, he cherishes you too much to leave you here. Carving out time for deep prayer when feeling you have come to the end of your personal strength allows him to help carry your burdens. And then prayerfully give yourself room to grieve and patiently work through this heartbreak. "Rejoice in our confident hope. Be patient in trouble, and keep on praying" (Rom. 12:12).

An act of betrayal may stem from many issues, including jealousy, insecurity, greed, fear, and a desire for power. Although they may not realize it, betrayal often reflects an attempt of the perpetrator to overcome their own deep-seated troubles. The one on the receiving end of a betrayal may feel shock, grief, lower self-esteem, anger, and self-doubt.[1] Does any of that ring true for you right now?

Betrayal can also feel like a stab in the back: we don't see it coming, and it causes immense pain. It tends to suck the joy out of our lives and throw us into a pit from which it is extremely difficult to escape. Know that, while you may feel completely desperate, isolated, and lonely, you are not alone. Many can relate to and empathize with your pain, which may feel all-consuming. Yet recovery and regaining your sense of self and worth are absolutely possible. Give yourself grace as you deal with the pain and work your way toward a brighter future.

Jesus suffered the greatest betrayal from one of his dedicated followers. After spending three intimate years learning from Jesus and being on mission with him as part of his inner circle, Judas gave him up to the Roman soldiers to be killed. The ensuing physical and emotional pain he endured, ultimately leading to his death on the cross, was horrific. Yet before the betrayal, Jesus, knowing what was to come, showed love and kindness to Judas. As he died on the cross, Christ also prayed for those who had nailed him there, saying they did not realize what they were doing (Luke 23:34).

While reflecting on his actions is helpful, Jesus's identity as fully God indicates that we can't possibly expect to hold ourselves to that standard of perfection. But we can learn that the ultimate goal, and the way to healing after a betrayal, is to begin the long and difficult journey to forgiveness. The negative feelings after a disloyalty can lead to ongoing relationship problems, including lack of trust, insecurity, wall building, anxiety, and isolation. These issues can bleed into relationships beyond the one with our betrayer. The effects of our suffering have the potential to create long-term struggles of identity, self-worth, and feeling desperately alone. I don't want that for you. God does not want that for you.

Healing from the deep wounds of disloyalty typically requires processing through the five stages of grief defined by psychiatrist Elisabeth Kübler-Ross: denial, anger, bargaining, depression, and acceptance. While we may want to rush through these steps to stop the hurt, allowing grace to work through each one will provide the opportunity for self-restoration and rebuilding trust in others. It is common to bounce among these steps rather than work through them in a sequential manner. And healing takes time, so patience during the grieving process will provide for ultimate healing.

In phase one, denial, we feel shocked and numb, doubting the reality of our situation. It's a defense mechanism that may initially help us cope with the discovery and survive the incident by minimizing the overwhelming pain. Emotions are typically very labile during this phase, ranging from tears to laughter to lashing out in anger.

It's important for us to feel and express all the emotions the betrayal has caused. Unfortunately, this suffering is unavoidable. It is also necessary since healing comes only as we work *through* the pain. Attempts to block or ignore the pain can lead to long-term physical, emotional, and spiritual damage. Journaling while processing the event and leaning on a trusted friend who is a great listener can be helpful methods in dealing with denial.

The next phase, anger, is marked by questions such as "Why me?" or "How could they?" Our anger, initially directed toward the betrayer, can spill over into sudden bouts of irritation toward things, friends, strangers, or family members. Experiencing anger is a normal and necessary step in the grieving process after a betrayal. It not only allows expression of the pain but also helps us begin to emerge from the isolation that occurs during denial.[2]

Finding a healthy outlet for the anger can help us feel saner and less volatile. Physical activities such as hiking, tennis, yoga, dance classes, or walking the dog provide a healthy alternative to internalizing anger. Anger art, in which emotions are poured out in a creative way, can be healing for others. Seeking help through a therapist, mindful meditation, or intense prayer can provide comfort and the opportunity for processing, healing, and growth. And it's OK to cry out to God in anger. He wants to walk through this valley with you. His unconditional love in these moments reminds you that you are valuable, worthy of love, and worth the journey to move through the anger toward wholeness.

During the bargaining phase of healing the wound of betrayal, we may begin to feel a sense of guilt or responsibility about the disloyalty. It can become a point of obsession as we replay all the events leading up to the discovery and try to determine our own role in the betrayal. Flight of ideas and rumination over details are typical in this phase and can lead to sleeplessness, decreased focus, anxiety, eating irregularities, and fatigue. We start to shift our internal questions to *What if ...?* or *If I do this, then will my life get back to normal?*

Self-criticism and self-blame are common during this period. We bargain for ways to lessen the deep emotional pain and to prevent future incidents that may cause similar grief. We may try to reimagine ourselves into a person who will never be the victim of a betrayal and can lose our authentic identity in the process. Regardless of your part in straining this relationship, you are *not* responsible for someone else's actions. While they may never take full ownership of the disloyalty, letting go of self-blame is absolutely fundamental to your healing.

Attention to self-care during this stage is critical. Finding ways to create a peaceful environment will support physical, emotional, and spiritual healing. Mindfulness, described in the appendix, helps us keep living in the present while looking toward a brighter future. Engaging in activities we have formerly enjoyed can help us begin to regain our identity and eventually restore joy. This may mean engaging in a hobby or participating in a gathering when we don't really feel like it. But with time, we can recapture the happiness we have once experienced from these events.

For some, the fourth phase, depression, can be the longest and most difficult one. It commonly overlaps the other stages and can leave us feeling exhausted, unloved, and alone. These feelings of extreme sadness are necessary in the route back to health. Because a betrayal indicates a loss of trust and, at times, a relationship, this grief-related emotion is expected. David Kessler, coauthor of two books with Kübler-Ross, describes the significance of this phase on the website http://grief.com: "We withdraw from life, left in a fog of intense sadness ... If grief is a process of healing, then depression is one of the many necessary steps along the way."[3]

The depression experienced in this phase can range from mild to severe. This, too, is a time to be dedicated to self-care. It helps to begin the day in prayer while crying out to God with all our hurt feelings. He sees us and knows every detail of what we are facing in this moment. Though anxious for the suffering to end, we must be patient in allowing him to show a way forward. Our heavenly Father hurts when we are hurting and wants nothing more than to bring us hope and restoration.

Intentionally seeking out fellowship with kind people who can provide moments of joy in our day can also help lift our spirits. As much as we may want to be alone in our pain, the genuine care of others can bring glimmers of light to our private darkness. And this is a time to unashamedly seek professional help. Therapy and medications have assisted many in successfully navigating depression and are not necessarily needed long term.[4]

The final phase, acceptance, does not automatically mean that all is well with the damaged relationship. It does mean that we have accepted the truth of the betrayal and have come to grips with this being our new reality. As we begin to have more good days than bad ones, we learn to readjust our perspective and find positives in moving forward. Acceptance allows us to acknowledge and let go of the past, live fully in the present, and look to a brighter future. While the healing process is difficult, it is here that we fully recognize our value and purpose and begin to reclaim our zest for life.

What stage of grief are you experiencing? Is it a combination of two or more? Be gentle with yourself and understand this is a natural response to the pain you are enduring from the betrayal. But please don't lose hope as you work through this ordeal. How can you incorporate one of the above self-care methods into your day? Pray for God to come alongside or carry you through this time and then make your healing the top priority for today.

This may sound impossible right now, and I get it. The emotions after a betrayal can be all-consuming. The wound is raw and gaping. But remember that nothing is impossible with God. He will provide the comforting salve to soothe your tender wound. When relied on, he will lovingly guide you through the necessary steps to repair and restore your mind, body, and spirit.

Reach out to your heavenly Father daily and be patient as he gradually carries you along the pathway to wholeness. While God loves you in all the brokenness that you are feeling right now, he doesn't want you to stay here. It is within you to be strong by surrendering to him when you feel like giving up. And he will faithfully walk by your side through each challenge ahead. Friend, it's time to dig in. I believe in you and pray for the healing of your fresh wound. You are worth this battle, and you are worth the journey to restoration.

VERSES TO ENCOURAGE YOU

When you go through deep waters, I will be with you. When you go through rivers of difficulty, you will not drown. When you walk through the fires of oppression, you will not be burned up; the flames will not consume you. For I am the Lord, your God.
—Isaiah 43:2–3

He heals the brokenhearted and bandages their wounds.
—Psalm 147:3

I will never forget this awful time, as I grieve over my loss. Yet I still dare to hope when I remember this: The faithful love of the Lord never ends!
—Lamentations 3:20-22

And he said to her, "Daughter, your faith has made you well. Go in peace. Your suffering is over."
—Mark 5:34

SONGS FOR YOUR SOUL

- "Can Anybody Hear Me" by Meredith Andrews
- "God Problems" by Maverick City Music
- "I Will Always Be True" by Third Day
- "Great Are You Lord" by One Sonic Society

A CONVERSATION WITH GOD

Dear God,

I cannot believe that this person I've trusted has hurt me so terribly. I feel angry, bitter, and sad. In my desperation, I have also questioned your love as I struggle to understand how you can let this happen to me. Why, God? Why? Fill me with your supernatural power to begin the process of healing. While I can't fathom it right now, help soften my heart to create an opening for forgiveness. As hard as it may be, help me make caring for myself a priority in this difficult healing process. Remind me of your love and faithfulness, even in my darkest hours. Amen.

NOTES

CHAPTER 33
When You Are Battling an Addiction

For the grace of God has appeared that offers salvation to all people. It teaches us to say "No" to ungodliness and worldly passions, and to live self-controlled, upright, and godly lives in this present age.

—TITUS 2:11-12 (NIV)

I f you are struggling with a dependence issue and have opened to this chapter, you have taken a huge and courageous first step. Acknowledging that you have developed an unhealthy habit requires honest, and often painful, self-reflection. It is within your grasp, however, to alleviate the hurt this addiction has caused you and others. And looking for help indicates a heart open to changing and healing. I pray that this chapter can help with the next steps to your recovery.

Looking back on his addiction, singer Elton John has said, "I realized that I only had two choices: I was either going to die or I was going to live, and which one did I want to do? And then I said those words, 'I need help. I'll get help.' And my life turned around." As he has learned, recovery from a dependence is best achieved with the caring and compassionate help of others. The acceptance of your struggle and reaching out for help can put you on a positive path to reclaiming your life.

Addiction is a common issue in our society. It often begins as something to help us cope but then eventually controls us. Our culture is brutal in this area as a primary marketing goal is not for us to simply like something but to become unable to do without it. We are bombarded by advanced audience targeting with ads and promotions directed specifically to our previous patterns and behaviors. Our weaknesses are exposed, and we become extremely vulnerable to suggestion.

It may have taken you a long time to open to this letter on addiction, and I am so thankful that you have. The word *addiction* alone can create feelings of denial or anger. While it's OK to feel those emotions, please don't let them keep you on the path of unhealthy choices. Begin by slowly breaking down your walls of pain and protection that have brought you to this point. I pray that you will feel God's presence and grace in the difficult yet ultimately incredibly rewarding days ahead. "For the grace of God has appeared that offers salvation to all people. It teaches us to say 'No' to ungodliness and worldly passions, and to live self-controlled, upright, and godly lives in this present age" (Titus 2:11–12, NIV).

Addiction is to be enslaved, bound, and powerless to something. It is the excessive use of something that damages health, relationships, jobs, and other parts of a normal life. Addictions can be physical, such as with drugs, alcohol (substance-use disorder), or food, or they can be behavioral. Behavioral addictions include gambling, sex, shopping, pornography, working, video games, and social media use.[1] The object of our obsession becomes the primary thing we obey, and the enemy loves for us to obey anything other than God.

The brain's natural response to a pleasurable experience is to release the neurotransmitter dopamine. Repetition of a behavior that causes dopamine release can over time result in dopamine secretion just in anticipation of that pleasurable activity. This increases the desire and urge to repeat the behavior that has triggered the pleasure pathway. Each time we indulge in the obsession and get a hit of dopamine, we are enforcing the positive biologic response.

This recurrent pleasure pathway stimulation increases the likelihood that we will repeat the pattern in the future. For many people who suffer from a dependency on something, there is an additional complication of not having an off button. Once the damaging behavior is started, they can't bring themselves to stop, even if there is a deep-rooted realization that the end result of engaging in the addictive behavior can have devastating consequences.

The statistics surrounding addiction are alarming. Almost twenty-one million Americans have at least one addiction. Drug overdose deaths have more than tripled since 1990. Over fifteen million Americans suffer from alcohol-use disorder, but only 7 percent will seek treatment. About 20 percent of Americans with anxiety or depression also have a substance-use disorder. According to the World Health Organization, up to 14 percent of college students report having a gambling problem. Nearly 18 percent of social media users experience addiction, and the majority of these are young single females.[2,3] These statistics are unfortunately just a small sample of the crisis.

When suffering from an addiction, we crave that habit or substance to the point of ignoring other vital areas of our lives. And no one is immune. Addiction can take the strongest people and reduce them to the point of feeling completely helpless and hopeless. Even if the subject of one's addiction is not inherently bad, it becomes a problem when it is expected to satisfy, soothe, and compensate for a void in life. We elevate the addiction on our priority list in an unhealthy way, using it to fill a gap. That gap may be between us and our partner, between us and the enjoyment of our job, between us and the stress of life, or even between us and God.

The first step in healing is to recognize and admit to the addiction. For those of us who may pride ourselves on independence and being in control, it is challenging to admit dependence on anyone or anything. And because the word *addiction* has a negative connotation in many people's minds, we don't want to acknowledge that it applies to us. Yet the importance of that acknowledgment cannot be overemphasized. The habits of sweeping the truth under the rug, being in denial, and making excuses deny us of the opportunity to begin the restorative process.

While the Bible may not specifically address addiction, it does remind us to respect our body, which is the temple for the Holy Spirit (1 Cor. 6:19), and not to give in to temptations (Matt. 26:41). Dependency on any earthly thing to bring hope and healing from our sorrows always results in disappointment and further brokenness. Relying on that behavior to satisfy our needs will never compensate for the one true satisfier of all our desires, God. It is through his love and grace that we can gain the needed perspective and fortitude to win the battle.

Addiction promotes the internal lie that God isn't enough to satisfy our dreams or to soothe our souls. It allows the enemy to convince us that "God can't, but this can." We fool ourselves into believing that the addiction is solving a problem for us when it is truly creating more troubles. We listen to the voice of the addiction when it tells us, *This is the only way,* or *At least this will help you feel better right now.* It takes great strength and determination to overcome these lies and the patterns of dependence or addiction. But we must believe that, with Christ, we *can* do this.

Your decision to read this chapter is a sign that you are ready for a change. This may be the first time you have had the courage to address the issue head-on. You may have made attempts in the past to discontinue the destructive behavior but eventually fallen into old patterns. You may even be extremely discouraged and doubtful that there is any hope for lasting recovery. But that is simply not true. You are taking a brave step right now, and the road to recovery always happens one step at a time. So hang in there and just focus on this first one.

Once you have admitted there is a problem, the next step is to identify why. What is the root cause of your addiction? Has there been unresolved trauma in your life that you don't want to think about? Is your reliance on this behavior providing an escape from something or someone? Are you feeling lonely, rejected, helpless, worthless, or driven by pride? What is the void you are trying to satisfy?

These questions require intense honesty and deep self-reflection. It can be painful and difficult to process. Delving into these tough issues often necessitates the assistance of a trained counselor or therapist. However, getting to the root cause is crucial to providing the opening for beginning the journey toward a lasting recovery.

Your heavenly Father loves you just as you are: bruised, scarred, and enslaved to the unhealthy behavior. But he loves you much too much to leave you there. He wants to see you fully healed. Accept that your addiction is preventing you from being the person God is calling you to be, both for yourself and others. If you have tried to recover on your own, consider seeking help this time. Invite someone into your struggle to give you guidance, support, and accountability. Whether it is a counselor or therapist, a trusted friend, or a mentor, this step is often highly beneficial, and in many cases crucial, to your ongoing success.

Actress Jamie Lee Curtis candidly spoke of the challenges she faced in battling dependency problems. She admitted that the work was painful and hard yet worth the struggle. This Academy Award–winning actress stated, "My recovery from drug addiction is the single greatest accomplishment of my life." She also described the importance of not trying to face the battle alone. "The help is there, in every town and career, drug-/drink-freed members of society, from every single walk and talk of life to help and guide." The chance for success is greatest when accomplished in community.

Friend, there are so many benefits of staying the course and fighting this battle. Studies have shown significant improvements in the quality of life for those in recovery. Your success can improve relationships, mental and physical health, and enjoyment of life. Additionally, the physiological craving and distress caused by the addiction will decrease over time.[4] The enemy wants you to believe that you are fragile and weak. While he wants you to believe the situation is hopeless, facts show otherwise. Know and trust that the power of Christ in you is stronger than the enemy.

In the Old Testament book of Nehemiah, we read about the Jewish people who had returned from captivity in Babylon to a Jerusalem in which the walls had been torn down and the gates destroyed by fire. The Jews were troubled, discouraged, and disgraced. As Nehemiah fervently prayed for them, he was given holy guidance and courage to approach the king to ask permission to rebuild the walls. With the compassionate king's permission, despite attempts of others to sabotage the mission, and through divine grace and power, the massive project was miraculously completed in just fifty-two days.

Your body, the temple for the Holy Spirit, has been damaged through this addiction. Your walls of self-protection have been torn down and the gateway to your soul destroyed. You may feel troubled, discouraged, and disgraced. Yet you have a powerful God waiting in the wings to help you rebuild your life, just as he helped Nehemiah rebuild the Jerusalem walls.

Despite the enemy's attempts to keep you enslaved to this behavior, your heavenly Father will show you the way to freedom. He will provide holy guidance and courage for you to overcome this stronghold. Escaping an addiction on your own is extremely difficult. But scripture offers proof that rebuilding, hope, and healing are possible when you choose to rely on our miraculous God.

Please don't wait another day to begin your battle. Follow through from this first brave step of looking for help. God is with you and for you. Pray for the wisdom to understand the truth of your destructive behavior and for the willpower to take the first steps toward regaining your life. Seek that trusted person to be your encourager and accountability coach. Know that a setback is not a failure but a stumble to propel you onward.

And remember: your loving Father is ready to stand in the gap for you and guide you forward as you work on breaking these chains. With God, you can courageously proceed and persist in this fight for freedom from your addiction. He will never leave you, even in the worst days of your recovery. Trust that there is a better life for you on the other side. Dispense with the enemy's lies and prove to yourself that the addiction can't, but God *always* can.

VERSES TO ENCOURAGE YOU

For I can do everything through Christ, who gives me strength.

—Philippians 4:13

You say, "I am allowed to do anything"—but not everything is good for you. And even though "I am allowed to do anything," I must not become a slave to anything.

—1 Corinthians 6:12

Keep watch and pray, so that you will not give in to temptation. For the spirit is willing, but the body is weak!

—Matthew 26:41

See, God has come to save me. I will trust in him and not be afraid. The Lord God is my strength and my song; he has given me victory.

—Isaiah 12:2

SONGS FOR YOUR SOUL

- "Freedom Hymn" by Austin French
- "Break Every Chain" by Tasha Cobbs
- "Rescue" by Lauren Daigle
- "Miracle Power" by We the Kingdom

A CONVERSATION WITH GOD

Dear God,

I am tired of allowing _____ to rule my life, but I am scared to stop. I want to lead a healthier life, yet I feel weak. Fill me with your strength and power, Lord. Protect me from the schemes of the enemy as he tries to thwart my efforts. Give me the will to persevere and the strength to succeed. When I stumble, Lord, give me the courage to get back up and continue forward. I know there is hope ahead as I break these chains. Thank you for loving me as I work to rebuild my life. Amen.

 NOTES

CHAPTER 34
When You Need to Show Compassion

Share each other's burdens, and in this way obey the law of Christ.

—GALATIANS 6:2

We live in an imperfect and broken world full of imperfect and hurting people. While it may be easy to get caught up in our own worries and sorrows or the demands and stresses of everyday life, helping other people with their burdens creates a win-win situation. In showing compassion to others, our mind is distracted from our own troubles while we care for someone through theirs. According to the Dalai Lama, love and compassion are not extravagances we can take or leave but rather are necessities in life.

Compassion has been recognized as a fundamental part of our humanity. Among emotion researchers, it is defined as the feeling that occurs when we are confronted with the suffering of another person that we feel moved to relieve.[1] It is a tangible expression of love that Christians describe as being the "hands and feet" of Jesus. "Share each other's burdens, and in this way obey the law of Christ" (Gal. 6:2). It is also the way to be the heart of Jesus by bringing hope to those who are suffering or struggling.

I am excited that you have opened this chapter. The desire and willingness to aid those in need speaks of your generous and loving character. While we can't hope to solve all the world's problems, it is possible to make a strong and positive impact in our community by showing compassion to those around us. The kindness, grace, and empathy that you bestow can begin an ever-widening ripple of hope.

Showing compassion to others has been found to have health benefits. Research indicates that when being compassionate, our heart rate slows, and we secrete oxytocin, known as the bonding hormone. Oxytocin release also has a calming effect such that it can lower stress and improve mental health. Imaging shows brain activity in the areas linked to empathy, caregiving, and feelings of pleasure when we are being kindhearted, leading to a desire to care for others.

Research has identified five elements to compassion.[2] First comes the recognition of suffering, which requires empathy and the ability to relate to another person. Second, one must understand the universality of suffering in the human experience. This requires opening our eyes and hearts to those around us, in our communities, and across the globe. The third element is feeling moved by, and connecting emotionally with, the distress of someone who is hurting. This step may go against the natural tendency of some who prefer to remain detached, but pushing outside our comfort zones in this area is essential.

Fourth is learning to tolerate the uncomfortable feelings expressed by others and those that arise within us as a result of their sharing. Becoming tolerant of the situation or resultant anguish is not the goal, though, as continuing to move against the cause of the distress is important to helping improve the well-being of the person in need. The final component of compassion is acting, or being motivated to act, to relieve the identified distress. It is in these acts of service that we can truly affect people and make a positive difference for God's kingdom.

Jesus modeled compassion throughout his ministry, even at times when others were outraged by his practices. One example of Jesus's kindness is in the Bible story about the woman caught in adultery in John 8:1–11. Jesus, clearly upset by the reactions and intentions of the crowd to stone her to death, showed compassion for the woman and defused the angry crowd with his calm and gentle demeanor. If we want to become more compassionate humans, we must pray that God will allow us to see the sufferings and needs of individuals or groups on whom we may have a positive impact and then ask for his gentleness to respond.

There are many times when compassion requires no action but rather just a kind, listening ear. Friends or family who need to vent don't usually expect us to change the situation. They simply need someone to hear and understand what they are going through. The opportunity to unburden themselves can allow for a much-needed emotional release. In these scenarios, trying to solve the problem or making suggestions of how they can solve it themselves may actually hinder their personal healing progress. The most effective support in these cases is providing a needed empathetic ear and perhaps a shoulder to cry on while the person processes their problems.

It is sometimes necessary to show compassion for others when their challenges are brought on by previous poor decisions. Acknowledging that we all make mistakes and letting go of the temptation to judge another in these circumstances also requires humility and kindness. Doe Zantamata, author of the *Happiness in Your Life* series, sums it up well: "It's easy to judge. It's more difficult to understand. Understanding requires compassion, patience, and a willingness to believe that good hearts sometimes choose poor methods. Through judging, we separate. Through understanding, we grow."

Compassion for others, tapping into that part of our human makeup, allows us to grow beyond ourselves and our personal wants and needs. It paves the way for change and benefits both individuals and society. In showing love by being the hands and feet (or ears) of Jesus, we also have the opportunity to increase our circle of influence.

You are in the current circumstance in which compassion is needed because God believes your kindheartedness will make a positive difference. These opportunities can be seen as divine appointments. What an honor to be entrusted with helping alleviate someone else's pain! While you may not feel prepared or equipped, your wise, heavenly Father knows otherwise. So, friend, heed the holy nudge and open your heart to showing compassionate care and understanding.

Author Steven Aitchison spurs us on with his encouraging wisdom: "The most powerful force in the world that can change the lives of millions of people is *compassion*." And it is in that show of compassion that God's kingdom is brought to the earth. What a blessing that you can participate in that venture.

VERSES TO ENCOURAGE YOU

Therefore, as God's chosen people, holy and dearly loved, clothe yourselves with compassion, kindness, humility, gentleness, and patience.
—Colossians 3:12 (NIV)

When he [Jesus] saw the crowds, he had compassion on them because they were confused and helpless, like sheep without a shepherd.
—Matthew 9:36

Don't look out only for your own interests, but take an interest in others, too.
—Philippians 2:4

Be kind and compassionate to one another, forgiving each other, just as in Christ God forgave you.
—Ephesians 4:32 (NIV)

SONGS FOR YOUR SOUL

- "Love Them like Jesus" by Casting Crowns
- "Give Me Your Eyes" by Brandon Heath

A CONVERSATION WITH GOD

Dear God,

At times, I am astounded by the painful situations of others, and sometimes I seem to miss the reality of their suffering. Jesus, grant me your eyes to see the hurting people around me. Give me your kind ears to listen to those who need to voice their burdens. And instill in me your gentle and compassionate heart to make a difference anywhere I can. In your perfect name, I pray. Amen.

NOTES

CHAPTER 35
When You Feel Joyful

Always be full of joy in the Lord.
I say it again—rejoice!
—PHILIPPIANS 4:4

Think about the beauty of a sunset, a blooming spring tree, a gentle snowfall, the smell of a fragrant flower, the hug of a child, or the laugh of a friend. God gives us these and many other wonderful gifts to make us happy. It gives him great delight when we laugh and smile. And one of the best parts of expressing joy is that being cheerful is contagious.

Author and spiritual leader Marianne Williamson has once said, "Joy is what happens to us when we allow ourselves to recognize how good things really are." Experiencing and exhibiting that joy is one way we can share God with those around us. When with someone who is upbeat and energetic, don't you find it easier to capture that positive energy and feel joyful too?

Hallelujah that you are in a joyful moment or season of life! This is cause for celebration and a reason to give gratitude to God. When you have been through difficult times, the jubilant ones are so, so sweet. Sharing your positive attitude, experience, and perspective with others can increase energy, enhance well-being, and even improve your overall satisfaction in life.

Hormones play a significant role in our ability to experience joy. The interactive and collective effects of endorphins, dopamine, serotonin, and oxytocin create the environment needed to experience happiness and optimism. Endorphins, neurotransmitters produced in the brain and pituitary gland, are associated with pleasure. Dopamine is released when we feel satisfied, happy, or excited. Some of the effects of the combination of these two chemicals are relaxation, pleasure, and motivation.

Oxytocin, sometimes referred to as the bonding hormone, is related to love and trust. Studies have shown oxytocin to cause a significant increase in trust and to positively affect social interactions.[1] Serotonin acts as a mood stabilizer and is associated with well-being and happiness. As you can see, the combination of these four neurotransmitters, sometimes referred to as the happy hormones, can create the optimal environment for our brains to be open to trust while we experience positivity and optimism.

God calls us to trust him and be filled with joy. What is the difference between happiness and joy? Happiness is an emotion that can be fleeting and may change from moment to moment. Joy, however, is more a state of being. Happiness lives in the moment, but joy rests in the soul. Happiness is a reaction to a situation, while joy transcends circumstances. Joy resonates deep within us: a sense of contentment, peace, or deep satisfaction. Joy cannot easily be shaken because it is part of the essence of who we are. Even in times of loss or sadness, our hearts can remain joyful.

Joy is mentioned numerous times in the Bible and is described in Galatians as a fruit of the Holy Spirit (5:22–23). As we love God and grow closer to him, surrendering our hearts and plans to his will, we gather these fruits, which enhance our lives. We are also told to always be joyful (1 Thess. 5:16) and to shout joyful praises to God (Ps. 66:1). It's clear that the Lord is passionate about our joy and desires for us to lead fulfilling lives.

Many Christians remember how it feels when we first accept Christ as our Savior. The moments when we fully comprehend and acknowledge that Jesus has died for us and still cares for us in everything we do brings indescribable delight. It is through understanding and living into those truths that we begin to experience a deep-seated, joyful serenity. This joy can be experienced in quiet solitude or in a room packed with people at a party. It is an intentional choice that requires practice, shapes our behavior, and determines our outlook on life.

Your life is full of challenges, stumbling blocks, and other trials. Your journey will certainly hold both terrific days and tough ones. Although you may not be happy in the trying times, you can choose to remain joyful. The knowledge that, even in those difficult times, God is with you and will continue to care for you can be a source of immense comfort and great joy. The dark seasons will pass, but his steadfast love will not.

Ah, friend, I am so grateful that you are basking in moments of triumph and happiness. Thinking of God's never-ending commitment can help you not sweat the small stuff that happens every day and appreciate these times even more. Your joyful heart is also beautifully infectious and will draw others to you. So today as you choose joy and live joyfully, share it with others. Shine your light, God's light, for all to witness. It is in this way that he brings a bit of his glorious heaven to those here on the earth.

VERSES TO ENCOURAGE YOU

But let all who take refuge in you rejoice; let them sing joyful praises forever.
—Psalm 5:11

Always be joyful. Never stop praying. Be thankful in all circumstances, for this is God's will for you who belong to Christ Jesus.
—1 Thessalonians 5:16–18

When I look at the night sky and see the work of your fingers—the moon and the stars you set in place—what are mere mortals that you should think about them, human beings that you should care for them?
—Psalm 8:3–4

Be glad in your God. He's giving you a teacher to train you how to live right—teaching like rain out of the heaven, showers of words to refresh and nourish your soul.

—Joel 2:23 (MSG)

SONGS FOR YOUR SOUL

- "Joy" by for King & Country
- "How Great Thou Art" by Caleb + Kelsey
- "What a Beautiful Name" by Hillsong Worship

A CONVERSATION WITH GOD

God Almighty,

I am amazed by the wonder of you and your creation. The reminders I have experienced today fill me with joy and awe at your constant goodness. Thank you for loving me exactly where I am in this moment. Knowing that I'm not perfect but am perfectly loved is an incredible gift that fills my heart to overflowing. Help me share this joy so that others may know you as well. Amen.

NOTES

CHAPTER 36
When You Need to Be a Peacemaker

Do all that you can to live in peace with everyone.
—ROMANS 12:18

Conflict with others is an unavoidable reality of life, and handling disagreements can at times be intimidating. While some personalities thrive on negative encounters, others shy away from confrontation at all costs. It is common to lie somewhere in between, and it takes loads of growth and maturing to learn to deal with conflict in a positive way. Becoming a vessel of peace in the face of confrontations brings hopefulness and an optimistic perspective that people may not otherwise experience.

Whatever the conflict you are experiencing, opening this chapter indicates your desire to bring positivity to a potentially damaging situation. What an awesome choice to make! Courageously stepping into a confrontation with the intention of being a peacemaker requires forethought, preparation, and patience. My prayer is that by the end of this chapter, you will feel better equipped to move confidently forward.

As the Dalai Lama notes, "The planet does not need more successful people. The planet desperately needs more peacemakers, healers, restorers, storytellers, and lovers of all kinds." Being a peacemaker is an act of love. Whether the dispute is between us and someone else or between two or more other individuals or groups, promoting peace in the face of conflict is both righteous and a valuable life skill. In the New Testament, Paul encourages, "Do all that you can to live in peace with everyone" (Rom. 12:18).

God calls all of us to be peacemakers, but what exactly does that mean? Being a peacemaker doesn't mean avoiding conflict nor always giving in. While we may feel strongly about a specific topic, event, or situation, the way in which we present our points can either escalate or defuse the intensity of the moment. Internal frustration and anger allowed to surface as hurtful or spiteful words may provide an immediate release of tension, but it will likely only hinder communication and escalate the problem.

Reconciling a relationship often requires both parties to be open and humble. Mark Leary, a professor emeritus of psychology and neuroscience at Duke University, describes *intellectual humility* as an awareness that one's ideas may be wrong. While people displaying this trait may have strong beliefs, they are also open to the ideas of others and more likely to be convinced that their own are wrong.

Research shows that intellectual humility is associated with curiosity, tolerance of ambiguity, and low dogmatism.[1] Understanding that few things in life are black and white creates the opening for potential compromise. These qualities help pave the way for mutual acceptance and ultimately constructive productivity through healthy conversations.

God calls us to be peacemakers, and the Bible provides wise instructions for handling interpersonal conflicts. In the New Testament book of Matthew, chapter 18, we are guided to first approach the person for a one-on-one conversation. This allows us to calmly address any misunderstandings in a private manner. If there is no resolution, we are then to bring one or two others into the fold to keep discussions honest and respectful. The final step, if all else fails, is to bring the conflict before church leadership to determine if they can assist in resolving the dispute. This can also mean presenting the situation to a mature, mutually trusted friend or confidant.

When experiencing interpersonal conflict, angrily lashing out in the heat of the moment is counterproductive. Instead, it's important to step back from the situation, take quieting breaths, and gain self-control.

Once in a state of composure, we can give ourselves time to process the other perspective. Allowing our frontal lobe (the reasoning center of the brain) to catch up with our amygdala (the emotional center of the brain) provides a better opportunity to rationally process the dispute.

Once we have had time to think through the issue wisely, we can then reach out to the other person. Taking the initiative to come together and seeking common ground may be the last things we want to do. Waiting for an apology that may never come, however, creates the potential for the internal frustration on one or both sides to rise to the point of no return. This constructive step of seeking commonality may require forgiving the other person despite how difficult they have been. But remember that Jesus has forgiven and died for us while we humans are a broken mess, modeling the path he wants us to take.

There are steps we can take spiritually to lessen our anxiety. We can bathe the situation in prayer before meeting with the other person, asking for God's wisdom in the situation and how to best approach the other side. Praying for a peaceful spirit during the conversation promotes the reality of bringing a calming effect to the meeting. If we are feeling fatigued, volatile, or angry, the meeting should be rescheduled for a later time.

A positive way to start the conversation is by acknowledging our role in the conflict. During the discussion, we must respectfully allow the other person to feel seen and be heard, validating the importance of their feelings and views. If the exchange begins to escalate with harsh words or shouting, we should take a step back, lower our voice, and calmly express the desire to resolve the situation peaceably. We may even need to put the conversation off to a later time to allow both parties to cool down.

One of the most difficult concepts for many of us to accept is that we don't always have to be right. Psychiatrist and author Gerald Jampolsky has coined the maxim "You can either be right, or you can be happy." Let go of the need to *be* right and focus on living right instead. Trying to perpetuate our point in the face of conflict will never lead to a peaceful resolution and isn't likely to make either side happy. Being a peacemaker requires putting others before ourselves. It often means choosing to reconcile a relationship rather than proving a point.

At times, being a peacemaker means acting as a mediator in the conflict of others. After praying for God's wisdom in the situation, we can approach both sides individually, offering to guide them to a peaceful solution. If both individuals or groups are agreeable, it is wise to begin the arranged meeting with a prayer, asking the Holy Spirit for open hearts and minds. During the discussion, as we listen to both parties, we should show equal kindness and respect and encourage them to do the same.

As the moderator, we need to make sure both perspectives are heard and feelings on both sides are validated. If tempers flare, we can use our gentle spirit to defuse and redirect the tension. Helping them see the other person and understand the source of their viewpoint separates the thoughts and ideas from the person presenting them. As we assist both sides in coming together to find common ground or a shared goal despite their differences of opinions, we begin to set the path to a peaceful resolution.

Promoting peace helps you and others embrace individuality. It takes differing views and detaches them from the individuals so that the debate over issues is not a personal battle. Being a peacemaker includes helping people reach a mutual understanding or shared reality. In doing so, disagreements over ideas or views can become a productive journey. The goal of the journey, though difficult at times, is to heal damaged relationships, restore harmony, and create a calm and mutually constructive environment.

When experiencing or witnessing conflicts, peacemaking may not be the societal norm, and it is often not the easiest way forward. Yet kudos to you; that is exactly what you have chosen. Your bravery in being a peacemaker has the potential to make a huge positive impact as others witness your selfless desire to make amends. Choosing peace is always God's way as he guides us to lead harmonious lives of love with others. And aren't the rewards always greatest when we walk in the wisdom of his way?

Singer, songwriter, and peace activist John Lennon has said, "Peace is not something you wish for. It is something you make, something you are, something you do, and something you give away." So go ahead, friend. Move courageously and lovingly forward in your efforts to bring peace and harmony to hurting people. I feel confident that, with God at your side, you can enormously affect the world around you in a positive and life-giving way. The benefits to being a peacemaker will likely be far beyond what you can imagine or even hope for. You've got this.

VERSES TO ENCOURAGE YOU

God blesses those who work for peace, for they will be called the children of God.

—Matthew 5:9

And let the peace that comes from Christ rule in your hearts. For as members of one body, you are called to live in peace.

—Colossians 3:15

So, if you are offering your gift at the altar and there remember that your brother has something against you, leave your gift there before the altar and go. First be reconciled to your brother, and then come and offer your gift.

—Matthew 5:24 (ESV)

SONGS FOR YOUR SOUL

- "Waymaker" by Michael W. Smith featuring Vanessa Campagna and Madelyn Berry
- "Make Us One" by Jesus Culture
- "Come to Jesus (Reconciliation Hymn)" by People of the Earth

A CONVERSATION WITH GOD

Dear God,

There is conflict brewing in my relationship, and I don't want that! I believe my view is the correct one, but why do I always feel the need to be right? Guide me, Lord, toward a path of humility. Help me be patient enough to see the other viewpoint. And most of all, create in me the ability to make peace where there is conflict, even if it means putting my own views and perspectives aside. Teach me to be like Jesus: patient, kind, humble, gentle, and seeking to bring people together rather than adding to the divisiveness in our world. It's in his precious name I pray. Amen.

NOTES

CHAPTER 37
When You Need to Be More Thankful

Thank the Lord! Praise his name! Tell the nations what
he has done.
—ISAIAH 12:4

The ancient philosopher Cicero has
once said, "Gratitude is not only the
greatest of virtues, but the parent of all others." So then all our morality
stems from living with an attitude of gratitude. But being thankful
isn't always easy, is it? The journey of life is filled with difficulties and
obstacles. When we are feeling fatigued, overstretched, overcommitted,
overworked, or underappreciated, it can be difficult to find reason to
give thanks.

In addition to the many obstacles we face in life, we also experience
a multitude of blessings. In fact, recalling the challenging parts of our
journey that we have overcome can help us recognize God's provision
and be grateful during difficult circumstances. Embracing the seasons
in which we can fully appreciate our blessings paves the way to an
overall more optimistic outlook. And intentionally cultivating gratitude
every day creates a positive energy that is infectious.

It requires self-reflection to realize when we are not being thankful
enough. That you have opened this chapter indicates a desire to
recognize and better appreciate God's generous provisions in your life.

Following this journey to gratefulness can not only bring an increase in your faith but also improve your relationships with others as you begin to appreciate them as some of life's greatest gifts. Once in the mode of gratitude, it is natural to want to share that joy. "Thank the Lord! Praise his name! Tell the nations what he has done" (Isa. 12:4).

A variety of research studies has shown that there are health benefits associated with practicing gratitude. In one study at the University of California San Diego School of Medicine, being grateful was associated with better sleep, better mood, less fatigue, and less inflammation in the body. Other studies have shown improved immune response and a variety of beneficial effects on the cardiovascular system. So living a life of gratitude actually is good for the heart![1]

The Bible's book of Psalms is a collection of praises, cries, and thanksgivings written by several contributors. King David has penned at least 73 of the 150 chapters and bears his heart through them. I love his authenticity with God about his joys and his woes. He unapologetically cries out to God in distress when feeling beaten and broken and openly praises him with thanksgiving when he recognizes God's provision. Even the psalms of despair typically turn to thanksgiving and hope in the end. We can use this same model in turning our sorrows to gratitude while glorifying God.

Lisa Appelo, author and widowed mother to seven children, has identified twelve benefits of giving God thanks.[2] These include both guarding us against the enemy and helping us see God in daily life. Satan's main scheme is to pull us away from God, therefore making us question his goodness. Being thankful not only draws us closer to God but also glorifies him as others witness our positivity.

Gratitude, according to Appelo, helps us live in the present rather than ruminating on past mistakes or worrying what tomorrow may bring. Being thankful for today's gifts and recognizing them as blessings from a loving Father deepens our faith and helps us walk in God's will for us. As we grasp the truth of the Lord's presence in our journey, we often experience a sense of peace, hope, and joy.

In your quest to become more thankful, I encourage you to start with three steps. First, verbalize your positivity. Communicating with others in a constructive way by sharing words of thanks can be life changing. By using social media, try sending out two or three communications of thanks each week. Not only will sending these messages help keep your spirits higher but it also lifts those of the reader or receiver. Additionally, you will be setting a positive example for anyone else who happens on your post.

Second, take time to appreciate your partner. Focusing on the positive aspects of those we are close to enhances our relationships and creates a more optimistic environment. Tell a family member that you love them and why. Write an old-fashioned letter or card of thanks and send it through the mail. You will light up that person's day when they read it. Sharing these types of words of affirmation strengthens the intimate bond we share with others.

Finally, one of the best ways to increase our ability to tap into thankfulness is to keep a daily gratitude journal. Write down three to five blessings for which you are grateful each day. Look for interactions with people that are special or meaningful. Learn to find small wonders in nature, such as a beautiful flower, the sound of rain, or the song of a nearby bird. When we choose not to take the moments of joy in our life for granted, we capture the opportunity to thank God every day for the beauty of the world and the people around us.

And God always wants to hear about your gratefulness. Instead of only running to God with prayer requests and when in need of help, praise and recognize him for all the small and big blessings you can be thankful for today. Even when you aren't feeling particularly joyful, the process of praying has been linked to a more positive overall attitude and improvement in health. Recognizing today's gifts helps you more fully trust in God's reassurances through difficult periods.

As pastor, author, and educator Charles Swindoll has said, "The remarkable thing is we have a choice every day regarding the attitude we embrace for that day." Upon awakening each morning, you choose what your mindset will be. You may not be in control of everything around you, but you do determine how to respond to the events that unfold. Swindoll goes on to say, "I am convinced that life is ten percent what happens to me and ninety percent how I react to it."

I encourage you to choose to seek out goodness and beauty in the people and the world you encounter today, my friend. Approach the world with a bright outlook and hopefulness. Decide to be a grateful and positive influence, providing encouraging light for those around you. This approach to vivacious living will energize you and those you touch. So today choose to live life with an attitude of gratitude. There is no doubt in my mind that you will be glad you do.

VERSES TO ENCOURAGE YOU

With praise and thanks, they sang this song to the Lord: "He is so good! His faithful love for Israel endures forever!"
—Ezra 3:11

Let them praise the Lord for his great love and for the wonderful things he has done for them.
—Psalm 107:15

Devote yourselves to prayer with an alert mind and a thankful heart.
—Colossians 4:2

SONGS FOR YOUR SOUL

- "Father I Thank You" by Jeremy and Adrienne Camp
- "Hallelujah" by Heather Williams
- "Thank You Lord" by Chris Tomlin featuring Thomas Rhett and Florida Georgia Line

A CONVERSATION WITH GOD

Dear God,

You have given me so much, and I often neglect to thank you. I am awestruck by the beauty of the mountains, the vastness of the oceans, and the wonderful sounds of nature. Thank you for these gifts. I am also grateful for the people you have put in my life and the ways in which you provide for me. Help me be a blessing to others as I gratefully accept what I have undeservedly been given. I pray all this in the name of the greatest gift of all, Jesus. Amen.

NOTES

CHAPTER 38

When You Want to Share God's Word

So, he went through all the town proclaiming the great
things Jesus had done for him.

—LUKE 8:39

A ccording to evangelist Billy Graham,
"Our faith becomes stronger as we
express it; a growing faith is a sharing faith." The thought of sharing our
faith or biblical scriptures with others, however, especially if they are
not Christians, can be intimidating and anxiety provoking. Many of us
choose the easy way out, the comfortable path, of not saying anything.
We may live out our faith, hoping others will take notice, but we don't
feel confident talking about it. Why put ourselves out there for potential
ridicule or judgment?

Or maybe we take the step of inviting someone to church with us.
This is a fantastic way to introduce someone to a community of believers
who can encourage them along their journey to accept Christ or grow
in their faith. We are then able to leave the scripture teaching and life
guidance up to the pastors and others we believe are more trained to
shepherd people along in their faith. Inviting someone to church may
make us feel a little uneasy, but it doesn't force us too far out of our
comfort zone.

But God doesn't ask us to stay comfortable in our faith. Being too relaxed can produce a stagnation in our own journey with Jesus. At times, we are called to move out of our comfort zones and do even more. After healing a demon-possessed man in Luke chapter 8, Jesus instructs the man to tell others about what God has done for him. Jesus tells the man to *share his testimony*. "So, he went through all the town proclaiming the great things Jesus had done for him" (Luke 8:39).

You, too, can make a profound impact on people by telling your personal testimony of faith. I am excited for you to gain confidence and courage in being a wonderful witness of how Jesus has affected your life. It's an awesome gift to give to others who may be hurting or feeling lost. You, my friend, can be a life-giving breath of hope by stepping outside your comfort zone and into the possibilities that God has in store for you as you courageously share.

A census of American religion conducted by the nonprofit Public Religion Research Institute in 2020 has revealed that 36 percent of young Americans, ages eighteen to twenty-nine, do not affiliate with any religion.[1] This is a staggering increase from 10 percent in 1986. These emerging adults tend to live out their faith differently from prior generations. Jenna Van Donselaar, a graduate of Yale Divinity School and former field organizer for Young Evangelicals for Climate Action, has challenged conservative-leaning churches who seemingly ignore progressive issues with their interpretation of the Gospel when she has said, "My faith is rooted in a call to social justice and a call to social action."[2] Because these young adults frequently value relationships over religion and people over platitudes, humbly sharing our testimony is often the best way to engage them. Leading them toward Christ results from emulating his radically unconditional love and acceptance.

As previously mentioned, we must understand that God doesn't call the equipped; he equips the called. The same God who has spoken us into awakening wants to speak to others too, and we may be the vessel of life-giving words he has chosen for this moment. What an incredible opportunity! When we are sharing God's word, we must remember to be warm, humble, and gentle. We cannot force the Gospel on people, and we cannot criticize nor condemn them into believing. We can only love them to Jesus and then trust him to do the rest.

When you feel the divine nudge or call to share your faith, it helps to be prepared. So let's take some time to logistically prepare for that opportunity. First, give thanks for being called to share your testimony with others. God obviously believes that your story is worth hearing. Bathe the process in prayer, asking him to reveal what the general theme of your testimony should be.

Ask God to recall to your heart and mind past experiences and challenges that have shaped your faith and trust in Jesus. What portions of your journey should you include? Prayerfully determine if there are parts of your walk best kept to yourself. Know that while sharing personal details is important, it is OK to keep some elements private as well.

Second, write it down. This process will help organize your thoughts and bring clarity to your story. Beginning with an outline can be helpful as you detail the parts of the story you intend to include. It also enables a higher level of thinking and more focused attention, both of which aid in remembering it later. Impactful testimonies typically include three elements: life before Christ, how you have come to Christ, and how Christ has changed or affected your life.

If you are struggling with where to begin, ponder the following questions: What has been missing in your life, and what methods have you tried unsuccessfully to bring fulfillment? Who or what circumstances have led you to contemplate turning to Jesus? What scriptures have you heard or read that have brought you hope and healing, and why have they been helpful? What are some of the specific ways God has shown up in your life since you have accepted Jesus? Complete your testimony with a statement of hope and the truth of eternal life for Christ's followers.

While some testimonies may have a huge turning point, others may reflect the consistency of God's presence throughout the person's life. Both are relevant, so never minimize the importance of your personal faith journey. Weave a meaningful scripture or two into the narrative, showing how God has spoken to you through his Word. Perhaps share your life verse, if you have one, and explain how it has guided you at various times. Great testimonies bring hope and encouragement and always point others toward Jesus.[3]

Trust that you have a story worth telling. God has created you, knows your journey intimately, and gives you purpose in sharing it. The past mistakes, challenges, and struggles that you prefer to keep hidden are all part of the rich tapestry that has brought you to the point of believing in and relying on our powerful God. Sharing personal, and sometimes painful, details gives credence to the narrative and persuades people to listen. Your authenticity and vulnerability help others understand the importance of your walk with Jesus.

It may not be easy to share your faith, my friend. It isn't always comfortable. But it is real. And God will use your story, *his* story, to influence others. So take the leap of faith to which the heavenly Father is calling you. Go in confidence and share your testimony gently and openly. Then watch God do his amazing work.

VERSES TO ENCOURAGE YOU

And he told them, "Go into all the world and preach the good news to everyone."

—Mark 16:15

And if someone asks about your hope as a believer, always be ready to explain it.

—1 Peter 3:15

Whoever believes in the Son of God has the testimony in himself.

—1 John 5:10 (ESV)

Come and listen, all you who fear God, and I will tell you what he did for me.

—Psalm 66:16

For God so loved the world that he gave his one and only Son, that whoever believes in him shall not perish but have eternal life.

—John 3:16 (NIV)

SONGS FOR YOUR SOUL

- "Salt and Light" by Lauren Daigle
- "My Story Your Glory" by Matthew West
- "My Testimony" by Elevation Worship
- "Whatever May Come" by Jeremy Camp and Adrienne Camp

A CONVERSATION WITH GOD

Dear God,

While amazed by your steadfastness in my life, I often find it difficult to share my faith. Thank you for calling me to be a voice for you in this world. Give me opportunities to share my faith and guide others to you. Lord, please provide the right words to create my testimony so that I can humbly and honestly share it with others. Grant me confidence in the moment that I may affect your kingdom in a positive way, bringing others to understand the beauty, wonder, and peace of a relationship with Christ. Amen.

NOTES

CHAPTER 39
When You Need Grace and Forgiveness

For the honor of your name, O Lord, forgive my many,
many sins.

—PSALM 25:11

Have you ever stood at the edge of an
ocean, taking in the vastness of the
water that goes beyond what vision can see? Closing your eyes, you hear
the melodic and rhythmic sound of the surf, sometimes a gentle cadence
and other times a fierce crashing of the sea. The ocean waves lap at
your toes, drawing you into its power. Songwriter Charlotte Eriksson
describes such a moment in her poem of the same name: "I will find
comfort in the rhythm of the sea."

But if you continue to stand in the surf without moving, the soft
sand will gradually build around your feet. With each rolling wave, it
feels as if you are sinking deeper and deeper into the seashore. Whether
seen in a photograph, in a movie, or in person, the sight and sounds of
an ocean can be quite magnificent and awe inspiring. Its vastness is a
reminder of the enormity of God, the wonder of his creations, and God's
limitless love for us.

We often don't feel worthy of God's never-ending love. Because we
are flawed and imperfect humans, we make mistakes—*many* mistakes.
And try though we may to be perfect while hopefully learning and

growing from our mistakes, we will continue to mess up. Sometimes the missteps affect only us. Other times, our words or actions wound others. When we recognize our errors, our slipups, our sins, we may begin to experience guilt and shame over our thoughts and behaviors.

The enemy wants us to wallow in the weight of our sins and failures. He wants us to give up on ourselves and God because that's how the enemy wins. But, friend, God doesn't ask you to come to him when you are perfect or without sin. Neither of those scenarios is possible while we walk the earth. He wants you to come to him now—broken, ashamed, and asking for mercy—so that he can fill you with his love and wash over you with forgiveness: "For the honor of your name, O Lord, forgive my many, many sins" (Ps. 25:11).

Recognizing the error of one's ways often leads to initial feelings of guilt, shame, and self-reproach. While sharing some of the same neural pathways, guilt and shame are distinct. Guilt occurs in response to a behavior that goes against our moral compass. Shame arises when we believe our reputation has been damaged by our actions. Social psychologist Daniel Sznycer teaches that guilt and shame are not bad emotions, even though we feel bad when facing them: "When we act in a way we are not proud of, the brain broadcasts a signal that prompts us to alter our conduct."[1] Thus, experiencing these emotions can help us make more beneficial changes going forward.

I am the worst sinner I know. Despite being a follower of Jesus, I fail miserably in trying to grow in likeness to him. At times speaking without thinking, I hurt people in the process. Regretting choices I make, I experience both shame and guilt over some of my words and actions. While it's encouraging to think there is some benefit to these emotions, I unfortunately continue to make mistakes every day. It leaves me wondering how God could possibly still love me when I am such a failure.

This is where divine grace comes in. The Reverend J. Patrick Street of Redeemer Church in Marion, Ohio, defines *grace* as "God's life, power, and righteousness given to us by unmerited favor."[2] Grace is an undeserved and unexpected offering from God to his people. It requires nothing from us. We cannot do anything to deserve or earn God's grace; it is a gift. It's a sign of his immense love for you and for me. God doesn't expect us to be perfect. Our failures, flops, and disappointments do not define us because we have a generous God who chooses to love us anyway.

We may be tempted at times to believe that, while God may still love us, he can't possibly forgive our actions. And yet he does. This is the awe of the Gospel: that *while we are sinners*, Christ has been tortured and died for us. Jesus has willingly borne the weight my sins and yours, and these sins have been nailed to the cross. "Father, forgive them, for they don't know what they are doing" (Luke 23:34). Jesus's death on that cross in Calvary erases the guilt of our past, present, and future sins. How can that possibly be true? Only through divine grace. Our loving God not only forgives but also persistently chases after us with his whole heart.

The message of grace is woven throughout scripture to provide reminders when we feel least deserving of God's love and forgiveness. It is in those exact moments that he welcomes us with open arms as beloved and blameless children. His compassion follows us from the moment we take our first breath until our final exhalation. This is symbolized by the fact that grace is also the topic of the last verse in the Bible: "May the grace of the Lord Jesus be with God's holy people" (Rev. 22:21).

You may be thinking, *OK, so maybe God does forgive me. But how can I forgive myself? How can I accept that I have wounded someone so deeply? How can I right the wrongs I have caused?* Are these questions you struggle with? Friend, please know your loving Father doesn't want you to live under the burden of tears and turmoil, but rather, he invites you to a freeing space of grace.

I understand the regret you are likely feeling in this moment. Can I encourage you to begin to seek healing right now by praying? As you thank God for his grace and forgiveness, pray for him to reveal the effect of your transgressions—not so that you can feel guilty but rather so you can understand the consequences of your actions, make a different choice the next time, and be open to his graciousness. Ask for direction. In his enormous love, God gives us the gift of the Holy Spirit. Despite our mistakes, we can trust this wise Counselor to show us how to promote healing and hope in ourselves and in others.

When our sins have affected someone else, restoration will often require meeting with the person we have wronged. Before the meeting, pray for strength and the right words for the situation. Pray to be a good listener as you allow the one you hurt to voice their perspective. Share regret at having caused them pain and ask for their forgiveness. Be honest, be open, be vulnerable, be genuine. While their initial response may be no, trust that your efforts have paved the way for healing to begin.

Now close your eyes and return to the vision of the sea, a solitary soul standing at the shore. Experience the limitless nature of God as you view the waters extending beyond where the eyes can see. Despite the apparent solitude, trust and comprehend that you are never truly alone. Jesus is standing right beside you. Can you visualize him there? Listen to the continual sounds of the surf, a beautiful reminder of God's everlasting love for *you*. It doesn't falter; it never stops.

Now take a few steps into the ocean, allowing the waves of God's never-ending grace to wash over you. It is a gift: undeserved yet freely given. As your feet sink deeper and deeper into the sand, picture sinking further and further into God's love. Let go of the guilt, my friend. Release it into the sea of love before you. Rid your mind of shame. And allow the truths of his amazing grace, eternal compassion, and complete forgiveness to fill you with peace.

VERSES TO ENCOURAGE YOU

May the Lord bless and protect you. May the Lord smile on you and be gracious to you. May the Lord show you his favor and give you his peace.
—Numbers 6:24–26

Are you tired? Worn out? Burned out on religion? Come to me. Get away with me, and you'll recover your life. I'll show you how to take a real rest. Walk with me and work with me—watch how I do it. Learn the unforced rhythms of grace. I won't lay anything heavy or ill-fitting on you. Keep company with me and you'll learn to live freely and lightly.

—Matthew 11:28–30 (MSG)

But God showed his great love for us by sending Christ to die for us while we were still sinners.

—Romans 5:8

So let us come boldly to the throne of our gracious God. There we will receive his mercy, and we will find grace to help us when we need it most.

—Hebrews 4:16

SONGS FOR YOUR SOUL

- "Even at My Worst" by Blanca
- "Ocean Wide" by the Afters
- "Known" by Tauren Wells
- "Broken Things" by Matthew West

A CONVERSATION WITH GOD

Loving God,

I come before you broken and ashamed, regretful that I have made yet another bad decision. Lord, I desperately need to feel the truth of your grace and forgiveness. Please give me the courage and strength to admit my wrongs and to humbly seek forgiveness from those I've hurt. I don't deserve your grace but am eternally grateful for it. Fill me with your love so I may pour that love out to others as I work to make amends. In Jesus's name, I pray. Amen.

NOTES

CHAPTER 40

When You Want to Worship God

Come let us worship and bow down. Let us kneel before
the Lord our maker, for he is our God.

—PSALM 96:6

W hat is worship? Some of us believe that worship is something we do on Sundays when we gather with other believers and sing hymns or songs about God. We may even choose the church we attend by the quality of the music team or by how the songs and lyrics make us feel. We may see worship as a way to prepare our minds and hearts to hear God's Word.[1] But in fact, worshipping God doesn't even require music. True worship is much more.

Worship is not about us. Worship is not something we receive but rather an offering to our gracious God, who is worthy of all our honor and praise. It is an attitude of the heart and a sacrificial act showing reverence to our Creator, the One who has sent his only Son to die for you and for me. He is Lord of lords and King of kings. In worship, with or without music, we stand before God and acknowledge his lordship over our lives. We display comprehension that he is deserving of our complete devotion. We praise him for giving us eternal life through Jesus Christ. Worship is a gift to our heavenly Father, who has given us so much.

As you recognize the circumstances that have brought you to this chapter, ponder the wonder of the Author of life, the Beginning and End of all things. Think about and verbalize his many attributes that sustain you and bring you hope. Thank him for his constant love and grace. *This is how we worship God.* "Come let us worship and bow down. Let us kneel before the Lord our maker, for he is our God" (Ps. 96:6).

Throughout the Bible, we hear stories of worship and encouragement to worship. David provides a faithful example of worshipping God through both trouble-free and challenging times. He writes, "O God, you are my God; I earnestly search for you. My soul thirsts for you; my whole body longs for you in this parched and weary land where there is no water" (Ps. 63:1). Despite difficulties, David continues to worship God by recognizing his power, glory, love, and protection. Throughout the Psalms, in times of both prosperity and defeat, we find King David authentically and unashamedly calling out to and worshipping the faithful Father.

Why should we worship God? In a highly recognized quote, author and speaker John Ortberg states, "I need to worship because without it, I lose a sense of wonder and gratitude and plod through life with blinders on." I don't know about you, but I never want to be blinded to the wonders of the divine Designer of the universe. In worshipping the one true God, we allow our minds to be filled with awe at his creations and provisions. We open our eyes to the intricacy of his workmanship, which is intangible and defies science. We acknowledge his power over all creation.

Despite being all-knowing and all-powerful, he is a wholly personal God. Through worship, we praise him for caring about the smallest details in our lives. We contemplate the wonder of God's love and dedication to each one of us, acknowledging he alone guides our destiny. We thank the Father for his continual provision and protection. While opening our hearts to him, the pursuer of our souls, we connect by inviting him to fill us with the Holy Spirit. Through worship, we wholeheartedly give ourselves back to God.

Sunrise is a time that often fills me with wonder at the beauty of God's creation. It signifies new beginnings, new mercies, and the chance for a fresh start. Sunrises bring hope and promise. Regardless of what yesterday has held, today begins anew with God's glowing orb cresting the horizon, filling the sky with hues only the ultimate Creator can design. The beauty in that moment calls my heart to worship.

While looking out over a lake at daybreak, I have noticed that the birds also seem to glorify the God of the sunrise. Ducks rest in droves together in the water during the night and through twilight. As the sun reaches the horizon, however, they slowly begin to take flight. Initially, only one or two ascend, but they are quickly joined by the remainder of the assembly. As the birds soar in circles across the warming dawn sky, they are united with other flocks and begin to sing. It feels as if they are singing to acknowledge the beauty of the moment and the wonder of their Creator. It seems that even the birds know the one true God merits worship.

So, friend, when you feel called to worship, rejoice. Bow down before the Holy One, for he alone is worthy of all blessing and honor and glory. He deserves your sacrifice, your humility, and your praise. Worship him through words, posture, songs, or journaling. Show gratitude for his consistency in your life—in both the hilltop moments and the valleys. Unblinded by the distractions of the world around you, reconnect with your Redeemer and Comforter, embracing this moment to give freely and fully of your time to him. Offer the gift of all that you are to the incredible God who has created you. He alone is worthy.

VERSES TO ENCOURAGE YOU

Therefore, I urge you, brothers and sisters, in view of God's mercy, to offer your bodies as a living sacrifice, holy and pleasing to God—this is your true and proper worship.

—Romans 12:1 (NIV)

How great you are, O Sovereign Lord! There is no one like you.

—2 Samuel 7:22

Give to the Lord the glory he deserves! Bring your offering and come into his presence. Worship the Lord in all his holy splendor.

—1 Chronicles 16:29

Blessing and honor and glory and power belong to the one sitting on the throne and to the Lamb forever and ever.

—Revelation 5:13

SONGS FOR YOUR SOUL

- "Is He Worthy?" by Chris Tomlin
- "Nothing Else" by Cody Carnes
- "Worthy" by Elevation Worship

A CONVERSATION WITH GOD

Dear God,

You are Alpha and Omega, the one true God. You are my Savior, Redeemer, Advocate, Avenger, Sustainer, and the Rock on which I can always stand. You are Lord of my life and lover of my soul. Thank you for the wonder of your creation, God, and the truth of your everlasting love and grace. May your Holy Spirit fill my heart and home as I bow down in worship to you, Lord. You alone are worthy! Amen.

NOTES

ACKNOWLEDGMENTS

To God: I am incredibly grateful to be your beloved child. I am in wonder and awe at your unconditional love, steadfast faithfulness, and miraculous power. I am in complete astonishment and eternal gratitude that you sent your Son, Jesus, to die for my sins, offering a life of grace. Thank you for calling me to this work and for not giving up on me when I wasn't sure if I should or could complete it. Thank you for persistently nudging me through those crashing waves of uncertainty that lasted over two decades, for gifting a beautiful place of peace for me to feel your unending waves of grace, and for the opportunity to continually reconnect with you in the deep to bring this work to completion. May each chapter bring the reader closer to you, and may the words of this book glorify *only* you, God.

To my husband, Jon: Thank you for being the kindest and most generous human I know. Your example has helped me be a better person, mother, wife, and friend. Thank you for believing in me and encouraging me to keep writing and keep listening to the divine nudges. Your continual love and support, even when it meant long weeks apart, are appreciated more than I can express. I am grateful for the wild journey of more than three decades we have been on together. From being lost in a jungle to sharing time in our happy place and everything in between... There is no one I would rather share my life with. I love you.

To Kayla: Thank you for your gentle nature in encouraging me to continue this project. Your support and assistance with edits, therapy wording, and citations have been hugely beneficial. Your kind, sweet nature is an inspiration and wonderful model for others. I love you dearly and am extremely proud that you are my daughter. Thank you for bringing Joe, an awesome son-in-law, to our family. Daniel is so lucky to have you both as his parents!

To Shae: Thank you for being a wonderful example of a Christ follower, always thoughtful of others and loving everyone fiercely. I so appreciate the writing course you have gifted to encourage me along this process and the prayers I know you have sent heavenward. The way you gently speak to and love *all* others well, even when they disappoint you, is an inspiration. Your selfless dedication to caring for those less fortunate is nothing short of amazing, and I cannot wait to see where God leads you in the years ahead. I love you and am incredibly proud to be your mama.

To Blake: You are a fun-loving and kind soul who makes me proud that you are my son. I love that you are unapologetically and uniquely you. It has been my honor to walk with you through times of challenge and to see you come out stronger. I am excited that you are on the path of your dreams and will continue to pray for God to hold you close and lead you in his best path for your life.

To the pastors and faith leaders who have poured into me: Your wisdom jump-started many of the topics and chapters addressed here. Your encouragement helped me see the light of Jesus in sometimes dark and troubled seasons. I am grateful that you each followed your calling and that God led me to you for instruction and to be reminded of his assurances.

To Dana and Laura: You were the first recipients of the original transcript twenty years ago. I am still devastated by the circumstances that led to sharing it but so grateful that God nudged me to step outside my comfort zone by giving it to you and put me in a place to offer words of encouragement. Thank you for saying it was helpful and that the writing offered the beginning to a long and thankfully successful road of healing. Your kind words helped spur me on in moments of self-doubt. May God continue to bless you with joy and hope in your renewed hearts.

To the Dive Deep Peeps: Thank you for all the love and support you have given and continue to give me in my walk of faith. You teach me, challenge me, laugh with me, and love me, even when our opinions may differ. It is an incredible honor and joy to be doing life with all of you, and I look forward to the years ahead as we share together all of life's joys and challenges.

To my circle of women of faith: Some are still walking this earth, and others have joined Jesus in heaven: Linda G., Linda B., Margo, Beth, Lisa, Sara, Tamara, Natalie, Pam, Andrea, Linda R., Nancy, Rhonda, Ally, Tobi, and others. I never realized how important and impactful having a posse of women who love Jesus could be until I joined my first life group and found an amazing woman mentor. Most of my adult life, from the age of thirty-two onward, has been shaped by your love for Jesus and for me. I am grateful for the different seasons in which God has placed you each in my life and for your words of wisdom, grace, and encouragement through the decades. Your steadfast pursuit of God, truth, and love has made me a better follower and child of Christ. I treasure each of you for your unique gifts and kind hearts.

To my editors, Keyren, Christa, Ashley, Valerie, and Kim: Thank you for the kind words and skilled guidance that were much needed for a newbie. Your time, energy, and expertise were greatly appreciated.

APPENDIX

PRACTICING MINDFULNESS

Mindfulness is defined as the quality or state of being aware of something. It helps us remain focused on the present, releasing yesterday's regrets and tomorrow's worries. It has been found to be a key factor in overall happiness. Intentionally incorporating mindfulness into our life can increase the ability to regulate our emotions while decreasing anxiety, stress, and depression. Because it improves general mental and physical well-being, many mental-health-care providers encourage utilizing this technique.

Begin by closing your eyes and bringing your thoughts to the here and now. Breathe slowly and deeply. Inhale for a count of five, hold for another five, and then exhale for the same duration. Notice the sensations in your body. Acknowledge the sounds around you, but don't allow them to pull your focus from your intention of remaining in the moment. Nonjudgmentally accept thoughts and feelings as they come, but then quickly release them and return to the present. Assess your body from head to toe, sequentially relaxing any muscles that feel tense or strained. Rest in this relaxed place for a few minutes, continuing to release any intrusive thoughts or feelings without judgment.

NOTES

INTRODUCTION: OPEN FIRST

1. "Good Good Father," track 1 on Chris Tomlin, *Never Lose Sight*, Sixstepsrecords, 2016.

CHAPTER 1: WHEN YOU FEEL AFRAID

1. "Five Things You Never Knew about Fear," *Northwestern Medicine*, October 2020, https://www.nm.org/healthbeat/healthy-tips/ emotional-health/5-things-you-never-knew-about-fear.
2. Tim Newman, "Dissecting Terror: How Does Fear Work?" *Medical News Today*, October 30, 2021, https://www. medicalnewstoday.com/articles/323492.
3. "Peace Be Still," track 5 on Hope Darst, *Peace Be Still*, Fair Trade Services, 2020.
4. "I Will Fear No More," track 2 on the Afters, *The Beginning & Everything After*, Fair Trade Services, 2018.
5. "No Fear," track 12 on Kari Jobe, *The Blessing*, Sparrow Records, 2020.
6. "Stand in Your Love," track 4 on Josh Baldwin, *Victory*, Bethel Music, 2019.

CHAPTER 2: WHEN YOU FEEL LIKE COMPLAINING

1. Shawn Achor, "Is the Glass Half-Empty or Half-Full?" *Success*, January 23, 2015, https://www.success.com/is-the-glass-half-empty-or-half-full/.
2. Barbara Johnson, *Stick a Geranium in Your Hat and Be Happy!* (Nashville, TN: Thomas Nelson, 1990).
3. "Grateful," track 11 on Elevation Worship, *There Is a Cloud*, Provident Label Group, 2017.
4. "Bring the Rain," track 8 on MercyMe, *Coming up to Breathe*, Fair Trade Services, 2006.
5. "Great Is Thy Faithfulness," track 5 on Jordan Smith, *The Complete Season 9 Collection (The Voice Performance)*, Universal Motown Records Group, 2015.

CHAPTER 3: WHEN YOU NEED TO FORGIVE SOMEONE

1. Lewis B. Smedes, *Forgive and Forget: Healing the Hurts We Don't Deserve* (New York: HarperCollins, 1991).
2. "Forgiveness," track 3 on Matthew West, *Into the Light*, Sparrow Records, 2012.
3. "Losing," track 4 on Tenth Avenue North, *The Struggle*, Reunion Records, 2012.
4. "Forgiveness," track 4 on TobyMac, *Eye on It*, ForeFront Records, 2012.

CHAPTER 4: WHEN YOU FEEL ANGRY

1. Raymond W. Novaco and Raymond DiGiuseppe, "Strategies for Controlling Your Anger: Keeping Anger in Check," *American Psychological Association*, 2011, https://www.apa.org/topics/anger/strategies-controlling.
2. "No Matter What," track 1 on Kerrie Roberts, *Kerrie Roberts*, Reunion, 2010.
3. "Anchor," track 10 on Skillet, *Victorious*, Atlantic Records, 2019.

CHAPTER 5: WHEN YOU FEEL ALONE

1. Brian A. Primack et al., "Social Media Use and Perceived Social Isolation among Young Adults in the US," *American Journal of Preventive Medicine* 53, no. 1 (2017): 1–8, https://doi.org/10.1016/j.amepre.2017.01.010.
2. Kendra Cherry, "Loneliness: Causes and Health Consequences," *Verywell Mind*, September 1, 2021, https://www.verywellmind.com/loneliness-causes-effects-and-treatments-2795749.
3. "I Am Not Alone," track 9 on Kari Jobe, *Majestic*, Sparrow, 2014.
4. "Never Walk Alone," track 6 on Hillsong Worship, *These Same Skies*, Hillsong Music and Resources LLC, 2021.
5. "Thank God I Do," track 1 on Lauren Daigle, *Lauren Daigle*, Atlantic Records/Centricity Music, 2023.

CHAPTER 6: WHEN YOU ARE TEMPTED TO BE UNTRUTHFUL

1. Suzanne Degges-White, "The Thirteen Essential Traits of Good Friends," *Psychology Today*, March 23, 2015, https://www.psychologytoday.com/us/blog/lifetime-connections/201503/the-13-essential-traits-good-friends.
2. "If We're Honest," track 8 on Francesca Battistelli, *If We're Honest*, Word, Fervent, 2014.
3. "We Won't Be Shaken," track 4 on Building 429, *We Won't Be Shaken*, Essential Records, 2013.

CHAPTER 7: WHEN YOU ARE TEMPTED TO BE UNKIND

1. "Social Comparison Theory," *Psychology Today*, https://www.psychologytoday.com/us/basics/social-comparison-theory.
2. "Speak Life," track 5 on TobyMac, *Eye on It*, Forefront Records, 2012.
3. "King of My Heart," track 3 on Kutless, *Alpha/Omega*, BEC Recordings, 2017.

CHAPTER 8: WHEN THINGS OR MONEY BECOME TOO IMPORTANT

1. "Why Giving Is Good for Your Health," *Cleveland Clinic*, December 7, 2022, https://health.clevelandclinic.org/why-giving-is-good-for-your-health/.
2. "American Dream," track 5 on Casting Crowns, *What If the Whole World Prayed*, Zoo Studio, 2002.
3. "Lose My Soul," track 13 on TobyMac, *Portable Sounds*, Forefront Records, 2007.

CHAPTER 9: WHEN YOU NEED ENCOURAGEMENT

1. Rick Warren, "Four Causes of Discouragement, and Four Cures," May 8, 2018, https://pastors.com/4--causes-of-discouragement-and-4-cures/amp/.
2. "You Say," track 5 on Lauren Daigle, *Look Up Child*, Centricity Music, 2018.
3. "By Faith," track 3 on 7eventh Time Down, *By Faith*, BEC Recordings, 2022.
4. "Fighting for Me," track 5 on Riley Clemmons, *Godsend*, Sparrow Records, 2021.

CHAPTER 10: WHEN PEOPLE ARE HURTFUL

1. Åse Marie Hansen, Annie Hogh, and Roger Persson, "Frequency of Bullying at Work, Physiological Response, and Mental Health," *Journal of Psychosomatic Research* 70 (2011): 19–27, https://doi.org/10.1016/j.jpsychores.2010.05.010.
2. Åse Marie Hansen et al., "Bullying at Work, Health Outcomes, and Physiological Stress Response," *Journal of Psychosomatic Research* 60 (2006): 63–72, https://doi.org/10.1016/j.jpsychores.2005.06.078.
3. Monica Frank, "Why Are People Mean? Don't Take It Personally!" *Excel at Life*, 2011, https://www.excelatlife.com/articles/meanpeople6.htm.

4. "Before the Morning," track 2 on Josh Wilson, *Life Is Not a Snapshot*, Sparrow Records, 2009.
5. "Even When It Hurts," track 7 on Hillsong United, *Empires*, Hillsong, 2015.
6. "Jesus Hold Me Now," track 10 on Casting Crowns, *Until the Whole World Hears*, Reunion Records, 2009.

CHAPTER 11: WHEN YOU NEED TO BE BRAVE

1. Margie Warrell, *Brave: Fifty Everyday Acts of Courage to Thrive in Work, Love, and Life* (Hoboken, NJ: Wiley, 2015).
2. "You Make Me Brave," track 1 on Bethel Music, *You Make Me Brave: Live at the Civic*, Bethel Music, 2014.
3. "Voice of Truth," track 3 on Casting Crowns, *Casting Crowns*, Beach Street Records, 2003.
4. "Confidence," track 4 on Sanctus Real, *Changed*, Framework Records, 2018.

CHAPTER 12: WHEN YOU NEED PHYSICAL HEALING

1. Feifei Qiu et al., "Impacts of Cigarette Smoking on Immune Responsiveness: Up and Down or Upside Down?" *Oncotarget* 8, no. 1 (2017): 268–84, https://doi.org/10.18632/oncotarget.13613.
2. Dipak Sarkar et al., "Alcohol and the Immune System," *Alcohol Research: Current Reviews* 37, no. 2 (2015): 153–55, https://www.ncbi.nlm.nih.gov/pmc/articles/PMC4590612/.
3. Obinna Nnorom-Dike et al., "Long Term Immunologic Consequences of Illicit Drug Abuse," *Journal of Alcoholism, Drug Abuse & Substance Dependence* 6 (December 9, 2020): 22, http://dx.doi.org/10.24966/ADSD-9594/100022.
4. Allison Pataki, "Chapter 15," in *Beauty in the Broken Places: A Memoir of Love, Faith, and Resilience* (New York: Random House, 2018): 93–99.
5. "Healing Hand of God," track 8 on Jeremy Camp, *Speaking Louder than Before*, BEC Recordings, 2008.

6. "In Jesus Name (God of Possible)," track 1 on Katy Nichole, *Katy Nichole*, Centricity Music, 2022.
7. "The Healing," track 13 on Blanca, *The Heartbreak and the Healing*, Word Entertainment, 2022.

CHAPTER 13: WHEN YOU FEEL WORRIED

1. *Mayo Clinic*, "Exercise and Stress: Get Moving to Manage Stress," Mayo Foundation for Medical Education and Research, August 18, 2020, http://www.mayoclinic.org/healthy-lifestyle/stress-management/in-depth/exercise-and-stress/art-20044469.
2. "I Will Fear No More," track 2 on the Afters, *The Beginning and Everything After*, Fair Trade Services, 2018.
3. "Truth I'm Standing On," track 4 on Leanna Crawford, *Leanna Crawford*, Story House Collective, 2020.
4. "The Answer," track 3 on Jeremy Camp, *The Answer*, Sparrow Records, 2017.

CHAPTER 14: WHEN YOU NEED TO HAVE MORE FAITH

1. Bible Study Tools, https://www.biblestudytools.com/lexicons/greek/nas/pistis.html.
2. "Promises," track 5 on Maverick City Music, *Maverick City Vol. 3 Part 1*, Maverick City Music, 2020.
3. "Stand in Faith," track 10 on Danny Gokey, *Jesus People*, Sparrow Records, 2021.
4. "Through All of It," track 10 on Colton Dixon, *Anchor*, Sparrow Records, 2012.
5. "There Was Jesus," featuring Dolly Parton, track 7 on Zach Williams, *Rescue Story*, Essential Records, 2019.

CHAPTER 15: WHEN YOU FEEL ASHAMED

1. Arlin Cuncic, "The Psychology of Shame," ed. Steven Gans, *Verywell Mind*, March 30, 2023, http://www.verywellmind.com/what-is-shame-5115076.

2. Shahram Heshmat, "Five Factors That Make You Feel Shame," *Psychology Today*, October 4, 2015, http://www.psychology today.com/us/blog/science-choice/201510/5-factors-make-you-feel-shame.

3. "Five Ways Shame Can Shape Your Life," *Clearview Treatment Programs*, February 13, 2018, http://www.clearviewtreatment. com/blog/5-ways-shame-can-shape-life/.

4. "Love Me like I Am," track 3 on for King & Country, *What Are We Waiting For?*, Word Entertainment, 2022.

5. "Any More," track 2 on CAIN, *Jesus Music*, Essential Records, 2023.

6. "Perfection," track 4 on Switch, *Better View, Part 1—EP*, Provident Label Group, 2021.

CHAPTER 16: WHEN YOU FEEL OVERWHELMED

1. "Learned Helplessness," *Psychology Today*, http://www. psychologytoday.com/us/basics/learned-helplessness.

2. Judith Orloff, "The Secret to Managing Being Overwhelmed," *Psychology Today*, October 31, 2016, http://www.psychology today.com/us/blog/emotional-freedom/201610/the-secret-managing-being-overwhelmed.

3. "Another in the Fire," track 10 on Hillsong United, *People*, Hillsong, 2019.

4. "I Lift My Hands," track 3 on Chris Tomlin, *And If Our God Is for Us ...*, Sixstepsrecords, 2010.

5. "Honestly, We Just Need Jesus," track 6 on Terrian, *Give It Time*, Gotee Records, 2024.

CHAPTER 17: WHEN YOU SEE AN INJUSTICE

1. LaTasha Morrison, *Be the Bridge: Pursuing God's Heart for Racial Reconciliation* (Colorado Springs, CO: WaterBrook, 2019).

2. Frank Newport, "LGBT Population in US Significantly Less Religious," *Gallup*, August 11, 2014, http://news.gallup.com/poll/174788/lgbt-population-significantly-less-religious.aspx.

3. "By Our Love," track 11 on Christy Nockels, *Life Light Up*, EMI, 2009.
4. "Proof of Your Love," track 2 on for King & Country, *Crave*, Fervent Records, 2012.
5. "We All Bleed the Same," track 5 on Mandisa, *Out of the Dark*, Sparrow Records, 2017.

CHAPTER 18: WHEN YOU WANT TO SHARE YOUR FAITH

1. Barna Group, "Almost Half of Practicing Christian Millennials Say Evangelism Is Wrong," *Barna*, February 15, 2019, http://www.barna.com/research/millennials-oppose-evangelism/.
2. "Give Me Faith," track 7 on Elevation Worship, *Kingdom Come*, Elevation Worship, 2010.
3. "Then Christ Came," track 10 on MercyMe, *Always Only Jesus*, Fair Trade/Columbia, 2022.
4. "Shine," track 2 on Newsboys, *Going Public*, Star Song Communications, 1994.
5. "My Story," track 2 on Big Daddy Weave, *Beautiful Offerings*, Fervent Records, 2015.

CHAPTER 19: WHEN YOU NEED TO HEAL A BROKEN RELATIONSHIP

1. Thomas Cory, "What Is a Toxic Relationship?" *HealthScope*, June 23, 2021, http://healthscopemag.com/health-scope/toxic-relationships/.
2. Melanie Greenberg, "Four Steps to Relationship Repair with the H-E-A-L Technique," *Psychology Today*, April 24, 2013, https://www.psychologytoday.com/us/blog/the-mindful-self-express/201304/four-steps-relationship-repair-the-h-e-l-technique.
3. "Come as You Are," track 6 on Crowder, *Neon Steeple*, Sixstepsrecords, 2014.
4. "Restore," track 5 on Chris August, *The Upside of Down*, Fervent Records, 2012.
5. "I Will Be Your Friend," track 4 on Michael W. Smith, *This Is Your Time*, Reunion Records, 1999.

CHAPTER 20: WHEN YOU FEEL MOVED
TO MAKE A DIFFERENCE

1. "Seven Surprising Benefits of Volunteering," *University of Sydney*, May 3, 2017, https://www.sydney.edu.au/news-opinion/news/2017/05/03/7-surprising-benefits-of-volunteering-.html.
2. Angela Thoreson, "Helping People, Changing Lives: Three Health Benefits of Volunteering," *Mayo Clinic Health System*, September 16, 2021, https://www.mayoclinichealthsystem.org/hometown-health/speaking-of-health/3-health-benefits-of-volunteering.
3. International Labour Office, *Global Estimates of Modern Slavery: Forced Labour and Forced Marriage*, 2017, https://www.ilo.org/wcmsp5/groups/public/---dgreports/---dcomm/documents/publication/wcms_575479.pdf.
4. Dutch National Rapporteur on Trafficking in Human Beings and Sexual Violence against Children and United Nations Office on Drugs and Crime, *Monitoring Target 16.2 of the United Nations' Sustainable Development Goals: A Multiple Systems Estimation of the Numbers of Presumed Human Trafficking Victims in the Netherlands in 2010–2015 by Year, Age, Gender, Form of Exploitation and Nationality*, https://www.unodc.org/documents/research/UNODC-DNR_research_brief.pdf.
5. "Do Something," track 4 on Matthew West, *Into the Light*, Sparrow Records, 2012.
6. "Hosanna," track 8 on Hillsong, *All of the Above*, Hillsong, 2007.
7. "God of Justice," track 7 on Tim Hughes, *Hold Nothing Back*, Sparrow Records, 2007.

CHAPTER 21: WHEN YOU NEED TO MAKE
AN IMPORTANT DECISION

1. "Seven Steps to Effective Decision Making," *University of Massachusetts–Dartmouth*, https://www.umassd.edu/fycm/decision-making/process/.
2. "Oceans," track 4 on Hillsong United, *Zion Acoustic Sessions*, Hillsong Music and Sources, LLC, 2013.

3. "Where You Lead Me," track 1 on MercyMe, *Undone*, Fair Trade Services, 2004.

CHAPTER 22: WHEN YOU WANT TO SING GOD'S PRAISES

1. Robert Emmons, "Why Gratitude Is Good," *Greater Good*, November 16, 2010, https://greatergood.berkeley.edu/article/item/why_gratitude_is_good.
2. "How Great Is Our God," track 3 on Chris Tomlin, *Arriving*, Sixstepsrecords, 2004.
3. "Your Great Name," track 8 on Natalie Grant, *Love Revolution*, Curb Records, 2010.
4. "Promises," track 5 on Maverick City Music, *Maverick City Vol. 3 Part 1*, Maverick City Music, 2020.

CHAPTER 23: WHEN YOU ARE STRUGGLING WITH PRIDE OR FEEL LIKE BOASTING

1. Gary Chapman, *The Five Love Languages: The Secret to Love That Lasts* (Woodmere, NY: Northfield Publishing Group, 2015).
2. Elizabeth Bernstein, "When Is It OK to Brag?" *Wall Street Journal*, December 5, 2016, http://www.wsj.com/articles/when-is-it-ok-to-brag-1480953723.
3. Preston Ni, "Eight Signs of a Narcissistic Communicator," *Psychology Today*, July 12, 2020, https://www.psychologytoday.com/us/blog/communication-success/202007/8-signs-narcissistic-communicator.
4. Bob Goff (@bobgoff), "Next time you're tempted to boast," Twitter, June 14, 2018, 11:11 a.m., http://twitter.com/bobgoff/status/1007279442253643776.
5. "Lay Down My Pride," track 4 on Jeremy Camp, *Restored*, BEC Recordings, 2004.
6. "Empty Me," track 4 on Chris Sligh, *Running Back to You*, Brash Music, 2008.

CHAPTER 24: WHEN NOTHING SEEMS TO BE GOING RIGHT

1. "Why Is the News Always So Depressing? The Negativity Bias, Explained," *The Decision Lab*, https://thedecisionlab.com/biases/negativity-bias

2. Barbara L. Fredrickson and Robert W. Levenson, "Positive Emotions Speed Recovery from the Cardiovascular Sequelae of Negative Emotions," *Cognition and Emotion* 12, no. 2 (1998): 191–220, https://doi.org/10.1080/026999398379718.

3. Steven J. Shabel et al., "GABA/Glutamate Co-Release Controls Habenula Output and Is Modified by Antidepressant Treatment," *Science* 345, no. 6203 (September 19, 2014): 1494–98, https://doi.org/10.1126/science.1250469.

4. Jordan Lee Dooley (@jordanleedooley), "Can I admit something?", Instagram photo, March 22, 2023, https://www.instagram.com/p/CqG4luDPu5P/?igshid=YmMyMTA2M2Y=.

5. "God Is in This Story," featuring Big Daddy Weave, track 3 on Katy Nichole, *Katy Nichole*, Centricity Music, 2022.

6. "Whatever May Come," track 5 on Jeremy Camp and Adrienne Camp, *The Worship Project*, Sparrow Records, 2020.

7. "Brighter Days," track 3 on Blessing Offor, *Brighter Days*, Sparrow Music, 2022.

8. "Hills and Valleys," track 4 on Tauren Wells, *Hills and Valleys*, Reunion Records, 2017.

CHAPTER 25: WHEN YOU NEED TO ENCOURAGE OTHERS

1. Steve Lawry and Erica Lawry, "Parakaleo Biblical Counseling," *Parakaleo Christian Ministries*, https://web.stanford.edu/group/parakaleo/about.html.

2. Paul Tripp, "How to Be an Encourager," *Paul Tripp Ministries*, July 17, 2019, https://www.paultripp.com/wednesdays-word/posts/how-to-be-an-encourager.

3. "Fighting for Me," track 5 on Riley Clemmons, *Godsend*, Sparrow Records, 2021.

4. "Something in the Water," track 1 on Carrie Underwood, *Greatest Hits: Decade #1*, Arista Nashville, 2014.

5. "I Will Follow," track 2 on Chris Tomlin, *And If Our God Is for Us ...*, Sixstepsrecords, 2010.

CHAPTER 26: WHEN YOU FEEL SAD OR ARE IN DESPAIR

1. Richard Powers, *Bewilderment: A Novel* (New York: W. W. Norton & Company, 2021).

2. Nancy Schimelpfening, "The Chemistry of Depression: What Is the Biochemical Basis of Depression?" ed. Steven Gans, *Verywell Mind*, January 5, 2021, https://www.verywellmind.com/the-chemistry-of-depression-1065137.

3. "I Will Carry You," track 10 on Ellie Holcomb, *Canyon*, Ellie Holcomb, 2021.

4. "By Your Side," track 3 on Tenth Avenue North, *Over and Underneath*, Reunion Records, 2008.

5. "Scars," track 4 on I Am They, *Trial and Triumph*, Essential Records, 2018.

6. "Don't Lose Heart," track 3 on Steven Curtis Chapman, *Still*, Provident Label Group, 2022.

CHAPTER 27: WHEN YOU ARE TEMPTED TO JUDGE OTHERS

1. Alaric Hutchinson, *Living Peace: Essential Teachings for Enriching Life* (Cowichan Bay, BC: Earth Spirit Publishing, 2014).

2. Rubin Khoddam, "Why Judging Others Is Bad for You," *Psychology Today*, May 6, 2015, https://www.psychologytoday.com/us/blog/the-addiction-connection/201505/why-judging-others-is-bad-you.

3. "Open the Eyes of My Heart," track 5 on Michael W. Smith, *Worship*, Reunion Records, 2001.

4. "From the Inside Out," track 5 on Hillsong, *United We Stand*, Hillsong, 2006.

CHAPTER 28: WHEN YOU ARE TEMPTED TO GOSSIP

1. Sophia Gottfried, "The Science behind Why People Gossip—And When It Can Be a Good Thing," *Time*, September 25, 2019, http://time.com/5680457/why-do-people-gossip/.
2. "If We Are the Body," track 4 on Casting Crowns, *What If the Whole World Prayed*, Beach Street Records, 2002.
3. "Stay Strong," track 10 on Newsboys, *The Greatest Hits*, Sparrow Records, 2007.

CHAPTER 29: WHEN YOU ARE CALLED TO BE A LEADER

1. Graduate programs staff, "The Five Qualities All Successful Leaders Have in Common," *Northeastern University*, January 24, 2019,_http://www.northeastern.edu/graduate/blog/top-5-leadership-qualities/.
2. Raj Sisodia and Michael Gelb, *The Healing Organization: Awakening the Conscience of Business to Help Save the World* (New York: HarperCollins Leadership, 2019).
3. "Rise Up (Lazarus)," track 2 on CAIN, *Rise Up*, Essential Records, 2021.
4. "Confidence," track 4 on Sanctus Real, *Changed*, Framework Records, 2018.

CHAPTER 30: WHEN YOU WANT TO BE GENEROUS OR SERVE OTHERS

1. University of Notre Dame, "Science of Generosity," 2009, http://generosityresearch.nd.edu.
2. Elizabeth Svoboda, "Scientists Are Finding That We Are Hard-Wired for Giving," *Science of Generosity*, University of Notre Dame, September 5, 2013, http://generosityresearch.nd.edu/news/hard-wired-for-giving/.
3. "Why Giving Is Good for Your Health," *Cleveland Clinic*, December 7, 2022, http://health.clevelandclinic.org/why-giving-is-good-for-your-health/.

4. Lisa Firestone, "The Benefits of Generosity," *HuffPost*, June 13, 2014, http://www.huffpost.com/entry/the-benefits-of-generosit_b_5448218?guccounter=1&guce_referrer=aHR0cHM6Ly93 d3cuZ29vZ2xlLmNvbS8&guce_referrer_sig=AQAAAMgvf1K K75XSR-4JgY8Fu3e0fT-Oc6MFylkkMOhgmKURIXFc9B6hut xdvpw41zD8I9nq5rsUcNQ74TmsVhdXiYdzUPsm0bZzfr49nlv rv6eYs-gwVI2a6Itmdv2wkriGmQ9ffkN6cLkv-RXwqwC8LPQ-Ys5wMCpWHmjGgr8rkA4o.

5. "I Refuse," track 3 on Josh Wilson, *See You*, Sparrow Records, 2011.

6. "Send Me Out," track 11 on Fee, *Hope Rising*, Fair Trade Services, 2009.

7. "God of Justice," track 7 on Tim Hughes, *Holding Nothing Back*, Sparrow Records, 2007.

CHAPTER 31: WHEN PRAYERS SEEM TO GO UNANSWERED

1. C. S. Lewis, *Christian Reflections* (C. S. Lewis Pte Ltd., 1967, 1980). Extract used with permission.

2. C. S. Lewis, *How to Pray: Reflections and Essays* (C. S. Lewis Pte Ltd., 1967, 2018). Extract used with permission.

3. "Haven't Seen It Yet," track 3 on Danny Gokey, *Haven't Seen It Yet*, Sparrow Records, 2019.

4. "Plans," track 4 on Rend Collective, *Whosoever*, Capitol CMG, 2022.

5. "Great Is Thy Faithfulness," track 5 on Jordan Smith, *The Complete Season 9 Collection (The Voice Performance)*, Universal Motown Records Group, 2015.

CHAPTER 32: WHEN YOU HAVE BEEN BETRAYED

1. S. Rachman, "Betrayal: A Psychological Analysis," *Behaviour Research and Therapy* 48, no. 4 (2010): 304–11, https://doi.org/10.1016/j.brat.2009.12.002.

2. Sandra S. Casabianca, "Mourning and the Five Stages of Grief," *PsychCentral*, February 11, 2021, http://psychcentral.com/lib/the-5-stages-of-loss-and-grief#anger.

3. Elisabeth Kübler-Ross and David Kessler, "The Five Stages of Grief," *Grief*, http://grief.com/the-five-stages-of-grief/.

4. Women of Rebirth and Therapeutic Healing (WORTH), "Betrayal Trauma Stages of Grief," http://lifechangingservices.online/worth/betrayal-trauma-stages-of-grief/.

5. "Can Anybody Hear Me?" track 3 on Meredith Andrews, *As Long as It Takes*, Word Entertainment, 2010.

6. "God Problems," track 6 on Maverick City Music, Chandler Moore, and Naomi Raine, *The Maverick Way Complete*, Tribl Records, 2023

7. "I Will Always Be True," track 8 on Third Day, *Revelation*, Essential Records, 2010.

8. "Great Are You Lord," track 1 on One Sonic Society, *Great Are You Lord*, Essential Worship, 2016.

CHAPTER 33: WHEN YOU ARE BATTLING AN ADDICTION

1. Mara Tyler, "Recognizing an Addiction Problem," *Healthline*, January 12, 2018, http://www.healthline.com/health/addiction/recognizing-addiction.

2. National Institute on Alcohol Abuse and Alcoholism, "Alcohol Facts and Statistics," US Department of Health and Human Services, 2021, http://www.niaaa.nih.gov/publications/brochures-and-fact-sheets/alcohol-facts-and-statistics.

3. Nathan Yerby, "Addiction Statistics," *Addiction Center*, September 23, 2021, http://www.addictioncenter.com/addiction/addiction-statistics/.

4. John F. Kelly et al., "Beyond Abstinence: Changes in Indices of Quality of Life with Time in Recovery in a Nationally Representative Sample of US Adults," *Alcoholism: Clinical and Experimental Research* 42, no. 4 (2018): 770–80, https://doi.org/10.1111/acer.13604.

5. "Freedom Hymn," track 2 on Austin French, *Wide Open*, Fair Trade Services, 2018.
6. "Break Every Chain," track 7 on Tasha Cobbs, *Grace*, Motown Gospel, 2013.
7. "Rescue," track 2 on Lauren Daigle, *Look Up Child*, Centricity Music, 2018.
8. "Miracle Power," track 6 on We the Kingdom, *We the Kingdom*, Sparrow, 2022.

CHAPTER 34: WHEN YOU NEED TO SHOW COMPASSION

1. "Compassion Defined," *Greater Good*, University of California Berkeley, http://greatergood.berkeley.edu/topic/compassion/definition.
2. Jenny Gu et al., "An Empirical Examination of the Factor Structure of Compassion," *PLOS ONE* 12, no. 2 (2017), https://doi.org/10.1371/journal.pone.0172471.
3. "Love Them like Jesus," track 5 on Casting Crowns, *Lifesong*, Reunion Records, 2005.
4. "Give Me Your Eyes," track 1 on Brandon Heath, *What If We*, Reunion Records, 2008.

CHAPTER 35: WHEN YOU FEEL JOYFUL

1. Michael Kosfeld et al., "Oxytocin Increases Trust in Humans," *Nature* 435 (2005): 673–76, https://doi.org/10.1038/nature03701.
2. "Joy," track 2 on for King & Country, *Burn the Ships*, Word Records, 2018.
3. "How Great Thou Art," track 10 on Caleb and Kelsey, *Worship*, Rhodes Records, 2018.
4. "What a Beautiful Name," track 5 on Hillsong Worship, *Let There Be Light*, Hillsong, 2016.

CHAPTER 36: WHEN YOU NEED TO BE A PEACEMAKER

1. Mark R. Leary et al., "Cognitive and Interpersonal Features of Intellectual Humility," *Personality and Social Psychology Bulletin* 43, no. 6 (2017): 793–813, https://doi.org/10.1177/0146167217697695.
2. "Waymaker," featuring Vanessa Campagna and Madelyn Berry, track 4 on Michael W. Smith, *Awaken: The Surrounded Experience*, Rocketown Records, 2019.
3. "Make Us One," track 6 on Jesus Culture, *Love Has a Name*, Jesus Culture, 2017.
4. "Come to Jesus (Reconciliation Hymn)," track 6 on People of the Earth, *Hope Is Here*, WeArePOTE Records, 2020.

CHAPTER 37: WHEN YOU NEED TO BE MORE THANKFUL

1. P. J. Mills et al., "The Role of Gratitude in Spiritual Well-Being in Asymptomatic Heart Failure Patients," *Spirituality in Clinical Practice* 2, no. 1 (2015): 5–17, https://doi.org/10.1037/scp0000050.
2. Lisa Appelo, "The Power of Gratitude: Twelve Benefits of Giving God Thanks," *Lisa Appelo*, http://lisaappelo.com/the-power-of-gratitude-12-benefits-of-giving-god-thanks/.
3. "Father I Thank You," track 4 on Jeremy Camp and Adrienne Camp, *The Worship Project*, Sparrow Records, 2020.
4. "Hallelujah," track 3 on Heather Williams, *This Time Around*, Fair Trade Services and Columbia, 2011.
5. "Thank You Lord," featuring Thomas Rhett and Florida Georgia Line, track 2 on Chris Tomlin, *Chris Tomlin and Friends*, Sparrow Records and Capitol CMG, 2020.

CHAPTER 38: WHEN YOU WANT TO SHARE GOD'S WORD

1. "The 2020 Census of American Religion," *PRRI*, July 8, 2021, http://www.prri.org/research/2020-census-of-american-religion/.
2. Mya Jaradat, "America's Youth Are Religious. They're Spiritual. But They Don't Trust Institutions," *Deseret News*, November 6, 2021, http://www.deseret.com/faith/2021/11/6/22752617/america-

youth-religious-spiritual-mistrust-institutions-unaffiliated-social-justice-chris-stedman.

3. "What Is Christian Testimony? How Do I Tell My Own Testimony Story?" *Unfolding Faith*, 2018, http://www.tyndale.com/sites/unfoldingfaithblog/2019/07/24/what-is-christian-testimony-how-do-i-tell-my-own-testimony-story/.

4. "Salt and Light," track 11 on Lauren Daigle, *How Can It Be*, Centricity, 2015.

5. "My Story Your Glory," track 1 on Matthew West, *My Story Your Glory*, Story House Collective, 2023.

6. "My Testimony," track 2 on Elevation Worship, *Graves into Gardens*, Elevation Worship, 2020.

7. "Whatever May Come," track 5 on Jeremy Camp and Adrienne Camp, *The Worship Project*, Sparrow Records, 2020.

CHAPTER 39: WHEN YOU NEED GRACE AND FORGIVENESS

1. Eve Glicksman, "Your Brain on Guilt and Shame," *Brain Facts*, September 12, 2019, http://www.brainfacts.org/thinking-sensing-and-behaving/emotions-stress-and-anxiety/2019/your-brain-on-guilt-and-shame-091219.

2. Rev. J. Patrick Street, "Pastor: What the Grace of God Does in Us," *Marion Star*, January 19, 2019, http://www.marionstar.com/story/life/2019/01/19/pastor-what-grace-god-does-us/2569447002/.

3. "Even at My Worst," track 3 on Blanca, *The Heartbreak and the Healing*, Word Entertainment, 2022.

4. "Ocean Wide," track 5 on the Afters, *Never Going Back to OK*, INO and Columbia, 2008.

5. "Known," track 6 on Tauren Wells, *Hills and Valleys*, Reunion Records, 2017.

6. "Broken Things," track 2 on Matthew West, *All In*, Sparrow Records, 2017.

CHAPTER 40: WHEN YOU WANT TO WORSHIP GOD

1. Ed Jarrett, "Why Should We Worship God?" *Christianity,* December 2, 2019, http://www.christianity.com/wiki/god/why-should-we-worship-god.html.
2. "Is He Worthy?" track 8 on Chris Tomlin, *Holy Roar,* Sixstepsrecords, 2018.
3. "Nothing Else (Live at Passion Conference)," track 14 on Cody Carnes, *Awe + Wonder,* TBCO Music, 2019.
4. "Worthy," track 6 on Elevation Worship, *Hallelujah Here Below,* Elevation Worship, 2018.

AUTHOR'S NOTE

If you are holding this book right now, know that you have been prayed over. My prayers are that anyone who has read portions of this book has found a strengthening of their faith, a renewal of their spirit, and a deepening in their relationship with God. I have referred to you as *friend* throughout this book not because I know each of you personally but because I trust that we are friends in Christ.

As Christians, we need a community of love and support to sustain and encourage us. The Bible reassures us that where two or more followers gather in his name, Jesus is present (Matt. 18:20). While you, the reader, and I make two, I want to inspire you to prayerfully consider widening your circle of faith. Be encouraged by the words in these chapters, the scriptures, and the songs. Then share that encouragement with others.

When you share your knowledge and heart of faith, it is amazing to see what the heavenly Father will do. Perhaps you will be inspired to write "open when" letters of your own to those you know and love. Perhaps you will feel more confident in reaching out to someone who is hurting. Don't miss the opportunity to make an impact for God and his kingdom while you are walking the earth.

I want to hear your stories as you find encouragement and ways to grow in your faith. When we deepen our relationship with God, it's hard to contain the enthusiasm we feel. So don't! Be encouraged and share the good news. I will be delighted to hear how you have been able to reassure others through God's Word at noeljansenbooks@gmail.com. You, my friend, are a blessing waiting to happen.

Printed in the United States
by Baker & Taylor Publisher Services